YOU START WITH ONE

o Floyd & Jane,

God's blessings on you both.

hank you so much for all you've

one in my life personally.

u always had confidence in me.

our encouragement and always caring

eans so much.

you're special people to me.

hanks for always being nice. In His Hope,

Deo

To

The men, women, and children who have supported our ministry with their prayers and finances so children like Lallani can hear the good news about Jesus.

Also, to the thousands of children currently in our program.

Published in Nashville, Tennessee, by Thomas Nelson, Inc., and distributed in Canada by Lawson Falle, Ltd., Cambridge, Ontario.

Printed in the United States of America.

YOU START WITH ONE

DEO MILLER
with Susan F. Titus

THOMAS NELSON PUBLISHERS
Nashville

In YOU START WITH ONE, the Miller's demonstrate how each of us can make a difference in one child and all of us together can change the course of a nation. All God asks of us is to do what we can, and almost all of us can help feed and clothe one child.

Dr. Gary L. Greenwald
Eagle's Nest Ministries

Never shall I forget the days spent with the Millers at "Hell's 17 Acres", where hundreds of boys and girls have come to a saving knowledge of the Lord Jesus Christ as a direct result of the care, concern, and compassion demonstrated by Deo and Elaine . . . It is as though one of the recipients of their ministry is saying, "God sent you from America to Sri Lanka. You built a bridge of love from your heart to mine, and the Lord Jesus walked across."

Dr. James Cunningham
Executive Director
International Christian Ministries

To know Deo and Elaine Miller is to know the children they feed . . . They are literally moved with compassion toward the hungry as Jesus was toward the lepers.

Happy Caldwell
Pastor, Agape Church
President, International
Convention of Faith Ministries

Contents

Foreword

In 1978, Deo and Elaine Miller embarked on a journey to Sri Lanka. It was supposed to be a part of a relaxing round-the-world junket—a sightseeing expedition that would, perhaps, yield some exciting slides to show to friends back home.

Some of the sights they saw, however, left permanent impressions, not on the film in their cameras, but on their hearts! Deo and Elaine were changed, not by the tours they took among glittering temples, but by chance encounters with the poorest of the poor in the ghettos of Colombo.

For less than half of the cost of throwing a pool party for a few friends in suburban Los Angeles, they found themselves giving half a village the first full meal it had seen in weeks. They saw the grateful smiles of children who could hardly remember the last time their stomachs were full. The Millers' consciences were disturbed every time they thought of turning their backs on those children, leaving them to hunger again. Their faith also was aroused as they thought of more ways God could enable them to help thousands of starving people in Sri Lanka.

Gradually, this successful construction magnate and his lovely socialite wife saw God opening a new door before them. It took courage to walk through that door, but once through it, Deo and Elaine found a new purpose for living and a host of adventures besides. Read on . . .

Don Richardson
Author of *Peace Child,*
Lords of the Earth, and
Eternity in Their Hearts

Acknowledgments

My special thanks to the late Dr. J. D. Carlson, noted pastor, author, and radio speaker for Missions to Children; the Reverend Art Beals, author, world missions leader, and missionary statesman; the Reverend George Crites, pastor and friend; Dr. and Mrs. James Cunninghan, missionary statesman, radio speaker, writer, and friend.

My gratitude is also extended to the following people for their spiritual insights and many years of encouragement and support: the Reverend and Mrs. Maurice Anderson; the Reverend and Mrs. Happy Caldwell; Dr. Gary Greenwald; the Reverend and Mrs. David Krist; the Reverend and Mrs. Coleman McDuff; the Reverend and Mrs. Syvelle Phillips; the Reverend and Mrs. Ronald Prinzing; Dr. and Mrs. Lester Sumrall; and the Reverend and Mrs. Delron Shirley.

Appreciation also goes to Wightman Weese for his relentless hours of editing.

Finally, my deepest level of gratitude goes to my wife, Elaine, for the many hours she spent helping me write this book and for being by my side in times of illness, despair, and the fight against hunger among the world's children.

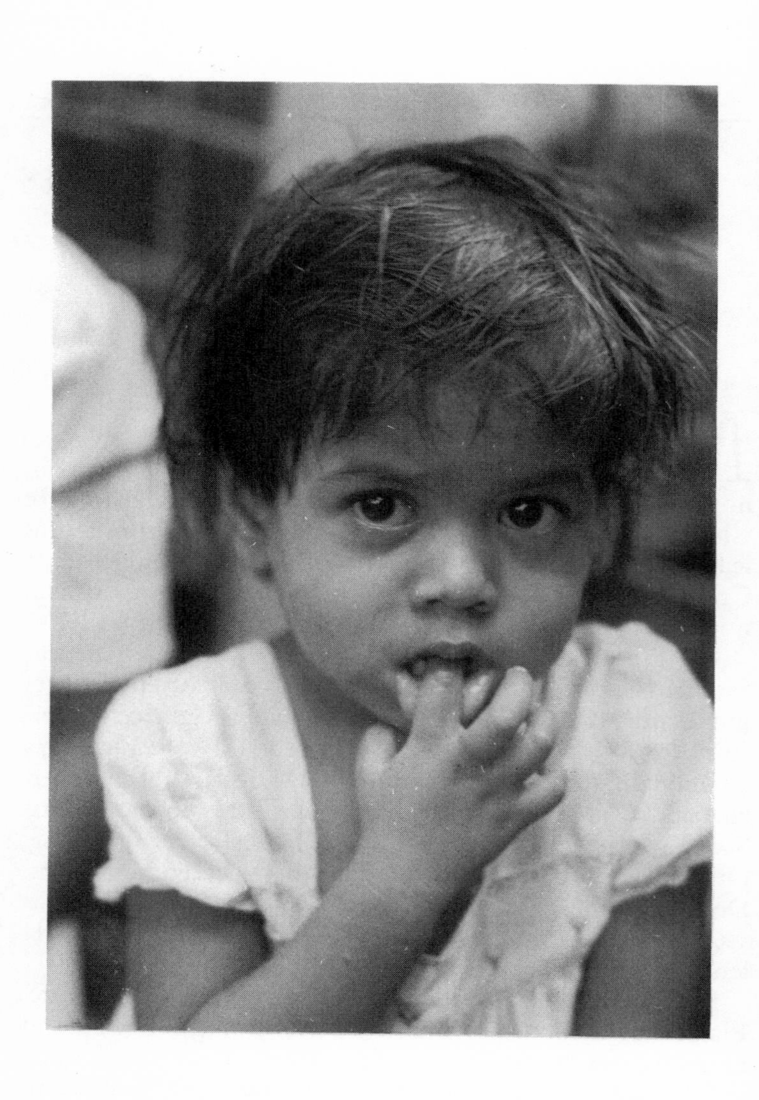

Chapter One

"We Can't Leave Her Here!"

It was our second day in the island country of Sri Lanka. The first sun rays blazed through the open window. The overhead ceiling fan lazily swooshed the humid air down onto our already moist bodies. Outside the window of our bedroom, squawking birds fought over a crumb.

I arose, quickly dressed, and walked onto the front veranda. Colton greeted me this morning wearing only a sarong. He clapped his hands. Immediately a servant girl appeared and was given instructions.

I thought back to my first meeting with Colton, when he spoke at our church in California eight years before. On that occasion he gripped the pulpit with his small, bony hands and waited for silence. Standing only five feet tall, Colton had worn a white suit with a mandarin collar, the custom for Sri Lankan pastors. His stark white suit made his cocoa skin glow. His beaming smile and twinkling, almond eyes radiated friendship.

His thinning hair, graying at the temples, was combed straight back. A neatly trimmed mustache added an air of distinction to the minister.

"My country is one of the poorest in the world," he had said. "We are unable to grow sufficient rice and must import more than half of our food. Our children, instead of asking, 'What are we having for dinner?' ask, 'Are we having dinner?'"

This little man of deep faith told us that day of his ministry in Sri Lanka, a country dominated by the Buddhist and Hindu religions. We heard of how God used him as an instrument to bring Christianity to the tiny island of Sri Lanka, which means "The Beloved Land."

Something in the pastor's presence seemed to transfix the congregation seated before him. He continued to speak of his cherished Sri Lanka, although he never appealed for money to buy food or clothing for the needy people, living on the streets and alleyways, that he described.

On this first meeting with Colton, my wife Elaine and I felt strangely attracted to the tiny but powerful man. He became a welcome guest in our home on each of his subsequent visits to the United States.

Each time he left us with the same invitation. "Come to Sri Lanka. Come to Sri Lanka. It's the Garden of Eden." But we always found some reason for not accepting.

Later, I invited Colton to be one of the officiating pastors for our daughter Danah's wedding. At the reception, he once again made the compelling request, "Come to Sri Lanka. Come visit me this March."

Again, I tried to make excuses; but he replied, "I came to perform the marriage ceremony for your daughter. Now, you promise to be my guest this spring." And so I felt obliged to make a commitment in front of our friends at the reception.

Here we were, several months later, guests in Colton's home. In a matter of minutes, the servant returned to the veranda, carrying a pot of tea and a tray arrayed with all kinds of fresh fruits. Crisp, pink guavas, greenskinned mangoes, and papayas were especially refreshing in the morning heat.

During breakfast, Colton's tone became solemn. "A cyclone hit the tip of the island a few days before you arrived. The villagers didn't see it coming and took no precautions, unfortunately. Members of the Sri Lanka churches have prepared fifty thousand packs of emergency supplies to distribute among the homeless. Deo, it would be so good of you to go with me today."

Cautiously, I smiled at my friend. "And my assignment, if I should choose to accept it, is to help you hand out the emergency supplies." I doubted, as soon as I had said it, that he recognized my allusion to the old TV show, "Mission Impossible."

"When you're finished with breakfast, we'll be on our way."

I went back to the bedroom, told Elaine where I would be going, and returned, dressed casually for the occasion. Little did I know how long and hard the trip would be, or how much the journey would change my life. Sri Lanka is 220 miles long and 140 miles wide. Most Americans remember it by its former name, the island of Ceylon. The tip of the island where we were going was about a hundred miles away. Again, I noticed that the tires on Colton's Volkswagen were worn slick as bicycle innertubes.

I asked, "Are you sure these will get us there?" Perhaps it would be "mission impossible" after all.

"Oh yes, yes," he said, smiling.

As we left the city behind, the bumpy road paralleled the Indian Ocean. Rolling waves broke in foaming surf along the deserted milk-white beaches. On the left side of the highway, coconut groves and rice paddies blanketed the countryside. A water buffalo, totally immersed except for its head and the tip of its back, blinked sleepily at our van as we rumbled past.

A profusion of jasmine and orchids carpeted the open fields and clung to the low branches of the trees. The sweet nectar of the frangipani blossoms drew hundreds of bees. Waxy-looking flowers of the iron trees looked so artificial, I wondered if they would melt in the sun.

Soon the flatlands turned to emerald velvet hills. Women, dressed in multicolored saris, labored on the terraced fields, golden bracelets dangling from their arms.

The workers were busy picking large, green leaves, tossing them in wicker baskets they carried on their backs.

"Tea leaves?" I asked.

"Yes," Colton answered. "Sri Lanka is the world's largest exporter of tea. Tea, rubber, and coconut are the mainstay of our economy. Half the earnings come from tea."

"I see many rice fields too," I commented.

"Yes, but it's not enough. Even with all these plantations you see along the road, one-half of our country's food must be imported. We have 15.6 million people here. Sri Lanka is one of the most densely populated areas in South Asia. They plow the rice paddies with water buffalo and harvest the crop by hand. There are no tractors. Also, more than half of the commercial agriculture is owned by foreign companies and individuals."

Our conversation ceased as we approached the area hit by the cyclone. Naively, I expected to see a few trees blown down, maybe a few houses damaged a little. How much damage could high winds do to such an immense jungle? When I arrived, I recoiled in shock at the devastation stretching before me.

Violent wind and driving rain from the tropical storm had swept over the coconut trees and nearby plantations, leveling everything in its path. Thousands upon thousands of coconut palms lay beside the gaping holes that once held the roots in position. Now, they looked like dead soldiers, lying unburied beside their own graves.

The small village that once nestled in the security of the giant coconut palms had been totally destroyed. Not one thatched-roof shanty was left standing. One elderly woman sat on the ground next to the few splinters that remained of her home. She rocked back and forth, clutching her knees and moaning in a thin, shrill voice.

Everywhere people aimlessly searched the rubble, hoping to find something useful for their families. One woman clutched a tin can she had found intact. Others held bits of cloth or broken plates. Nothing of value seemed to have survived.

As we walked along the devastated beach, children followed us. One little boy pleaded, "Rupees. Rupees, please." I will never forget his big, brown eyes staring at me.

Dirty little hands reached up, tugging at my shirt. I looked down into the face of a young girl. She said softly, "Mister, I'm hungry."

I was overwhelmed, realizing that I had no way to meet all their needs. Sadness gripped my heart. The thought *Surely, someone should do something about all this suffering* went through my mind over and over.

Soon other pastors arrived. Colton greeted them and gave the order to begin unloading the "Soup, Soap, and Salvation" emergency packets.

In a few hours we had distributed 50,000 packets, handing them out on a first-come-first-served basis. After the supplies were depleted, people continued to walk up to us with outstretched arms. I estimated 200,000 whom we were unable to help. The horror of the experience was reflected in their eyes. Then climbing sadly into the VW, we started the long trip back to Colombo.

The van bounced along the road. After a prolonged silence I asked, "Just what was in those packets?"

"Each one contained a yard of cloth, a bar of soap, a package of soup, a small straw mat, and a gospel tract. The cloth will protect them from the hot sun and the night ocean breezes. The mat will provide a bed, and the soap will help prevent the spread of infection. The soup will fill their stomachs, at least for a little while, and the gospel will offer them hope in their time of despair. That is why we call them, 'Soup, Soap, and Salvation' packs," he said.

"The need is so great . . ." I said, shaking my head.

"I agree," he said, nodding as he drove.

Physically we left the devastation behind, but I knew it would remain always in my heart. Driving back through the tropical jungle, I could still see the children's eyes, pleading and begging. A strong feeling of helplessness swept over me. We rode on in silence.

After a few hours the driver stopped near a small village so we could stretch our legs. I walked over to the side of the road and looked around. A boy pushing a cart filled with bananas greeted me. "Hello. Hello." Several girls strolled by carrying water jugs on their heads. They giggled and waved shyly. I smiled and waved back.

Suddenly, a few feet back from the road a movement caught my eye. There, crouched in the bushes, was a small girl about three years old. She was barefoot and wore a tattered, red and white gingham dress.

When I approached her, tears welled up in her big, brown eyes. They trickled down her cheeks, smearing her dirty face. Neither the boy in the cart nor the girls had seemed to pay any attention to her. How could this child not be noticed by those who walked by? Didn't anyone care?

I scooped her up in my arms and tried to comfort her. At first, she shook with fear as I held her close to my chest. I actually felt movement inside her bloated stomach that pressed against me, probably worms. Her ginger-colored hair was matted and falling out, symptoms of long-term malnutrition and hunger.

Colton walked over and stood watching me.

"Why would she be out here all by herself?" I asked.

"She has probably been abandoned. There are thousands more like her," he replied sadly.

I gazed into her enormous brown eyes, overwhelmed at her desperate situation. I spoke soothingly to her, although I knew she probably couldn't understand me. I continued to hold the child in my arms. She stopped shaking and lay her head on my shoulder. I looked at Colton who knew what I was thinking.

"How can I just walk away? We can't leave this little girl sitting here. I'd like to do something if I can!" I heard myself pleading.

Colton stared at me for a moment without speaking, as if in deep thought. Then he spoke slowly. "I'm sure some nearby families would be willing to take an extra child if someone would pay for her food. Most of these village people are poor, many with seven or eight children. They have difficulty feeding their own families. Taking in an extra mouth to feed without extra money would be impossible for them."

"I'd be willing to send some money every month to feed her. Could we find a home for her somewhere?"

Colton replied, "We can. And we will." He turned toward the van and I followed, carrying the tiny little bundle in my arms. Soon we stopped at the home of a pastor. I listened to Colton as he explained my proposition to pay for the child's upkeep. I gave a sigh of relief when I saw the pastor nodding his agreement. We left some money with him, with a promise of more soon to come.

I was almost reluctant to release the little girl. I watched from the VW as long as I could as we drove away. Long after we were out of sight, the little girl's eyes and dirty, tear-streaked face remained indelibly printed in my memory.

We continued our journey along the coast. Leaning back in the seat, rubbing my eyes, I realized just how exhausted I felt. I was glad to see Colton's house come into view.

Elaine and Suzanne, Colton's wife, had spent the day shopping in Colombo. During dinner, Colton and I told Suzanne and Elaine about the devastated village and of the thousands of homeless and hungry people we had turned away. Somehow words seemed inadequate to describe all the destruction and despair I had witnessed.

When Elaine and I went to bed that evening, I told her about the little girl. "I found her beside the road in the middle of nowhere," I said. "She was abandoned and starving. Elaine, I couldn't leave her there. I told Colton we'd pay for her food if he found a home for her. The local pastor is in the process of doing that now."

Elaine sat beside me on the bed listening quietly. "Relax.

You're tense," she said, rubbing my back. "You know I'm happy to support you in your decision. Anyway, how much can it cost to feed one little girl?"

I replied, "We can feed her for a whole day for the price of a cup of coffee! Surely I'm willing to give up one cup of coffee a day to keep a little girl alive!" A lump was forming in my throat, making it hard to speak.

Elaine looked at me quizzically. "What is bothering you?" she asked with what sounded like alarm.

I placed my arm around her and held her tightly. I was now trembling with emotion—almost like the little girl I had held just a few hours ago. "I don't honestly know, Elaine. I can't find the words to explain what I'm feeling."

But I think she knew. It was the little girl—and all the other things I had seen that day.

I was exhausted. Climbing into bed, I lay there trying to sleep, but couldn't. All kinds of questions and rationalizations filled my mind. I didn't come to Sri Lanka with the intention of becoming involved with helping these people. I simply came to visit a friend. Colton's earlier words kept ringing in my ear. "Come to Sri Lanka. Come to Sri Lanka. It's the Garden of Eden."

The next several hours I tossed and turned, but I kept seeing the penetrating brown eyes of homeless children I had seen all day. They stared at me expectantly. In my mind I saw their parents searching through the rubble for morsels of food, a jar, anything of value. I saw the towering palms flattened helplessly on the beaches.

Then the tearful eyes, the feel of the little girl trembling in my arms came back to haunt me. I had agreed to feed her—what more could I do? Why couldn't the government take care of these people? But that wasn't the answer, I knew.

I rolled out of bed and knelt on the floor. "Dear God, how can I help? I'm only one person." As I prayed my eyes filled with tears and my whole body shook as I thought about the suffering I had seen.

In my mind, I thought I could hear the answer. "These

people are your brothers and sisters. Their skin is a different color, and they speak a different language; but inside they are just like you. My Spirit can live in them, as I do in you. Deo, they are your responsibility also."

Glancing at the other side of the bed, I realized Elaine had been watching my struggle. She was weeping softly as she crossed the bed to kneel beside me. I took her in my arms and cried. "Oh, Elaine. This whole thing is too much. What can we do for these people? The need is so incredibly great. How can we help them? Where do we begin?"

Elaine answered, "Let's pray."

As we prayed quietly a wave of excitement came over me, a feeling of euphoria. I knew the answer to my question.

"We begin with one child. We'll start with this one little girl."

Elaine agreed. "Feeding one will be easy. Thousands seems impossible, but feeding one will be no problem. You're right. We'll start with one."

We looked at each other, and we both knew in that moment that our lives had been changed, and by a tiny little girl whose name we didn't even know. Peace swept over me. Now I thought I would be able to sleep.

Chapter Two

Outside the Garden of Eden

While I was drifting off to sleep, my mind reeled at how fast things had moved for us since the 747 jet had touched down less than 36 hours before.

I knew I would always remember the blast of heat that hit us as the door of the huge airliner swung open to a panoramic view of coconut palms swaying in the hot Indian Ocean breeze. On the edge of the runway, lush vegetation blanketed the hills with living green velvet. The smell of burning wood and curry filled the air.

At last we had arrived in Sri Lanka, the teardrop-shaped island that seemed to drip from the southern tip of India. Marco Polo had described this small country as the "finest island of its size in the world." It was later called the "Island of Serendip" by Arab traders, who imagined it to be a land of delight. Some claim that Solomon dispatched a ship to Sri Lanka to purchase peacocks and pearls for the queen of Sheba.

I took Elaine by the hand and guided her down the ramp landing. Brown-skinned men met us to carry our luggage. They smiled widely, motioning to a dusty Volkswagen van. Standing next to the vehicle was Colton, our dear pastor friend.

"Elaine! Deo! Oh, so good to see you! So good having

you here! You've finally come," he said, wiping his moist brow. His British accent was clear and sharply polished.

We had finally arrived to keep our promise, eight years after our first encounter with this little man of such great faith. As I gazed at the breathtaking scenery, I wondered why I had always found a reason for not visiting this beautiful land. And why did I have this strange feeling that this experience would somehow change my life?

Interrupting my thoughts, Colton shook my hand vigorously and gave Elaine an affectionate hug. "We will stop for lunch. I'm sure you're tired after the long flight."

The VW engine roared to life, and we left the airport behind. Colton instructed the driver in Sinhala, the predominant language of the island. Soon we were bumping along a narrow road hacked through the primitive jungle. We were on our way to a resort hotel, Colton explained. Eighty-foot palms towered in the sun, their giant fronds arching to form a vaulted ceiling above our heads. Noisy parrots bickered and chattered; their bright colors of green, red, and yellow looked as if someone had freshly painted them.

The vehicle wound its way deeper into the lush rain forest away from the capital city, Colombo. The narrow black strip of highway seemed to materialize out of nowhere from the green jungle that lurked on either side of the road. Men and women with gleaming white teeth, walking along the roadside, smiled and waved friendly greetings to us. Some of the women with long, black hair gracefully supported water jugs on their heads. Brown-eyed children ran after the van, waving and shouting in clipped British accents, "Hello. Hello."

Most men dressed in sarongs, long garments fastened around the waist like skirts. Some men wore collarless shirts, while others went bare-chested. A few dressed in western attire.

Nearly every woman wore a brightly colored sari. Later, we learned that they wrapped a six-yard piece of fabric around the body, pleating it in the front and draping it over the shoulder to form this beautiful dress. A few of the saris were made of silk, heirlooms passed down from mothers and grandmothers, Colton explained. The plainest woman looked beautiful wearing one of them.

These friendly, exotic people enchanted me. I felt strangely at home among them, though everything else about the environment seemed alien. I could not explain my feelings of camaraderie with every Sri Lankan I had met.

Suddenly, the driver stopped the van at the edge of a wide, meandering river. The three of us climbed out and surveyed the breathtaking view. We seemed to have been transported to deep within the jungle of a Tarzan movie. Dense, tropical plants and flowering trees lined both banks. Crocodiles sunned themselves on nearby rocks. Bright, yellow fish jumped out of the water. A spotted-billed pelican, his immense bill nearly as long as his body, swooped down and pocketed the fish for his dinner. Then he glided off once again into the blue sky.

Two teenage boys, rags tied around their waists, pushed toward us in a makeshift ferry. They dipped their bamboo poles in rhythmic unison as the raft glided across the algae-filled river.

"Come ride to the other side," one lean-hipped youth suggested in English. Since Sri Lanka was once the British colony of Ceylon, many of the people still spoke English.

The ferry was a simple row of wooden planks, loosely held together by rope woven from coconut husks. Water lapped in the large gaps between the planks as weight shifted on the raft. With trepidation, we climbed aboard. My weight caused the raft to rock and bobble like a cork. I could almost step through the holes between the planks that slapped up and down with each movement. I thought of the crocodiles behind us, sunning on the rocks. Elaine gripped my arm at the sight of them. Colton laughed at our uneasiness.

About midstream, we began to relax and enjoy the scenery. Wild birds called in the distance. In such a place so different from anything we could have imagined, time seemed to stand still. I looked up and prayed quietly. "Thank you, God, for such serenity, for such a gorgeous view!"

The raft thumped to a halt against the bank on the other side of the river. Colton gave the boys a few rupees for their labor. Gleaming smiles expressed their appreciation.

Gold-veined velvet orchids graced the steep path leading to the restaurant. The dark green jungle shimmered in the noontime heat. Tangerine-colored petals of the coral trees filled the air with their fragrance. Twisted roots of a snake tree appeared almost in agony. Lilac, crimson, and yellow vines crept up the trunks, intertwining in a colorful profusion. Nestled around the bases of the tree were hibiscus and bird of paradise plants.

A peacock danced with his plumage spread before his peahen near the entrance of the restaurant. Beautiful young ladies with their long black hair drawn back in tight buns greeted us with warm smiles and sparkling eyes. Seeing our white skin, they shyly bowed their heads when we spoke. They beckoned us onto the open veranda overlooking a bluish-green lagoon.

Our host ordered, and soon we were sipping tropical drinks made from the milk of the king coconut, enhanced by a hint of lime. The nectar quenched our parched throats.

Lunch arrived, and we tasted our first authentic rice and curry meal. Elaine took a bite and gasped, "Oh, this is hot! Quick, a glass of water!" Our host laughed.

I found the flavorful, hotly seasoned dishes delightful. Fried bananas, broiled fish, and rice seasoned with ginger, coconut, and hot pepper, with chutney served on the side made a delectable feast.

Small, red and yellow birds perched on the open-air windowsill, waiting for a crumb or a piece of rice. I gazed over the veranda at the meandering river, entranced by all the beauty around me.

Colton leaned forward in his chair. "Didn't I tell you it was a tropical paradise? It's the Garden of Eden."

Again, a strange unsettled feeling overcame me. I did not answer our host.

He stared at me for a while, then said, "I will take you to my home now." Clapping his hands, he called the waitress to bring the bill.

The young women smiled and shyly bowed their heads again. Softly in unison they chanted, "Cheerio. Cheerio. Tah. Please come back."

As we journeyed along the path back to the ferry, glowing butterflies darted among the trembling leaves of the stately trees. Colton's words, "It's the Garden of Eden," kept whirling in my mind. I wondered if Adam and Eve experienced a similar beauty.

At water's edge the boys waited for our return. They helped us back onto their rickety ferry and pushed hard with their long bamboo poles against the gentle current. Their broad-shouldered bodies glistened in the sun. "Why you come to our country?" one of them asked. "You like?"

"We came to visit our friend," was my response.

"You friend of this man?" the young boy asked, pointing to Colton.

"Yes, he is my friend and brother in Christ," I answered, wondering if he understood the meaning of my words.

The boy bowed his head and put two fingers in his mouth. Shyly he asked, "Can I be friend, too?"

Again, I felt overwhelmed by the amiability of these people. "Of course, you can be my friend," I answered, patting him on the shoulder.

We stepped off the raft and walked toward the VW. I glanced back and saw both boys grinning and waving. We entered the stifling van, and soon we were bumping down the road at what seemed an excessive speed. The roads in Sri Lanka were chunks of stone covered witha sticky layer of black tar. The nearly bald tires on Colton's VW gained little traction as we headed for Colombo.

We rounded a corner and startled an elephant. Peering

out from the edge of his domain, he raised his trunk and belted out a trumpet sound that declared his territorial rights.

Nearing the capital city, we felt transported back thousands of years in time. Carrying large bundles of goods on their heads, women returned home after shopping and trading in the open-air market, as they likely had done for centuries. Ox carts loaded with bananas and palm branch thatchings crept along the narrow road. Whenever the drivers heard the blast of a horn, they slapped their oxen with sticks. Slowly, the animals moved over to the side of the road, allowing the cars and trucks to pass. The rule of the road seemed to be that traffic flowed wherever it could squeeze through on the narrow roadway.

I watched a father and son push a cart filled with large bags of rice. The wheels wobbled slowly under the load that probably weighed close to a ton. Dark skins glistened in the bright sun as they strained in the sweltering heat to move the worn-out cart. Their toes gripped the cracks in the road surface trying to gain more traction. Looking up long enough to catch my eye, the boy smiled painfully as we drove by.

Finally we reached Colombo, which has one of the largest artificial harbors in the world. A few modern buildings loomed over the narrow, bustling streets. The van slowed to a crawl. Vendors hawked their wares, walking between the vehicles on the congested streets. Ancient bazaars offered bargains, herbal cures, and tea.

Colton warned us, "Keep your arms inside the van."

Busses passed within inches, blowing black diesel smoke into our open windows. The heat, fumes, and smell of unbathed bodies all mixed together. By now, my shirt was drenched with perspiration.

Elaine fanned herself with a magazine. Trying to sound pleasant, she asked Colton, "Is it always this warm?"

He replied, "This is the cool part of the year!" Everyone laughed.

However, the mood and the chattering in the van

changed as the stark reality of the area became apparent. Silently, I stared in disbelief. Adam and Eve suddenly seemed to be, as it were, thrown out of the Garden of Eden and into the world outside. Most of the people were in rags; children ran naked through the streets. Some were taking showers from buckets. Women and children scavenged through the rubbish for pieces of wood or paper to take back to their shanties for cooking fires. If this was, as Colton said, one of the poorest countries in the world, I shuddered to think there could be one worse.

Entire families lived and slept on the sidewalks. A feeling of their despair and hopelessness overcame me. Thoughts that defied words churned in my mind.

Elaine's eyes filled with tears, "You never told us this side of the story. Why?"

Colton reached over and patted her knee. "I was afraid you would not come to Sri Lanka if you knew the whole story," he answered softly. "Half of Colombo's population live in temporary housing. One million of the five million who make up the labor force are unemployed."

We drove on silently through the clamoring, crowded streets. Soon the driver came to the outskirts of the great port city. Zigzagging back and forth, we threaded our way along the winding road leading to Colton's home. A shimmering panorama of emerald grasslands, stately palms, and dense thickets surrounded us. Monkeys swung from tree to tree, scolding each other in high, shrill voices.

Suzanne, Colton's wife, greeted us with a gracious smile and open arms. "So nice having you here. Make yourselves comfortable on the veranda." Clapping her hands, she beckoned a servant to bring us something to drink.

The maid hurried to the kitchen, returning quickly with tall glasses of cucumber juice. Our first tropical drinks had tasted sweet. This was tart, but still delicious. I could feel the pulp on my tongue as the juice gave momentary relief from the oppressive heat.

Suzanne showed us to our room, modestly furnished by our standards. The clean bed looked inviting after our thirty-six-hour day on the plane. The sheets were turned down. Elaine and I took a short nap before dinner.

Hearing a slight tap on the door, I awoke to Colton's announcement, "We will be eating out this evening at a local hotel restaurant." Later, we learned that dining out for them was a rare occurrence.

Our table that evening overlooked the Indian Ocean. A soft, warm breeze blew across the open-air dining area, providing welcome relief. A foaming ocean pounded the beach below.

Colton said, "Until recently, Sri Lanka was known as the Hawaii of the Europeans. The numerous resorts and flower-drenched residential areas of the affluent are a legacy left by the British."

I could sense the old-world charm and the thin veneer of sophistication of this prestigious area of the city. But would I ever be able to erase the picture from my mind of the poverty I had seen on the streets of Colombo?

Colton continued, "The animosity between the easy-going Sinhalese and the hard-working Tamils has virtually stopped the tourist trade. Each outbreak of violence damages the country's fragile economy. I pray for peace and understanding for the people of my country."

Colton looked tired and appeared older than his fifty-two years. I realized what a toll the sorrows of his island country, so appropriately shaped as a teardrop, had weighed on the tender spirit of this loving pastor.

Colton's words swirled in my mind as I watched the sunset cast a reddish-orange glow across the horizon. It was a picture postcard setting, truly a tropical paradise. But what could be done for all those destitute people? I had no answer for my friend.

Dinner arrived. I was served a delicious seerfish, grilled with a wisp of coconut and curry flavoring. Before we were married, Elaine had modeled professionally. Much to her delight, a fashion show of the local women's apparel followed dinner.

"Tomorrow morning we'll come back, and I'll introduce

you to the designer of these clothes," Suzanne promised Elaine. At the time we had no idea what an important and meaningful part these fashions would play in our lives and what would result. Maybe we did have part of the answer for our friend Colton. We just didn't know it at the time.

As we left the restaurant, Colton took me aside and said in a serious tone, "Tomorrow I have something quite pressing to do, but it is on the tip of the island. I know you are tired now, so we'll talk about it in the morning."

"Sounds good. I'd like to see the other side of the island if I wouldn't be in the way," I answered with a feeling that Colton's words carried more meaning than I realized.

A short time later we returned to Colton's house where, despite the heat, Elaine and I collapsed in bed, hearing nothing till the sun rays filtered through our window the next morning.

"How did you sleep?" Colton asked after he had sent the servant girl for our breakfast. It was then that Colton told me of the pressing matter he had mentioned the night before at the hotel restaurant. Soon some of the emergency packets were loaded, and after breakfast we were on our way. As we drove along that morning, I asked Colton more questions about the economy of the country. It seemed too strange to me that a country that appeared so lush and fertile had so many poverty-stricken people.

"You would have to know the history of my country," he answered. "The Portuguese arrived here in 1505 and ruled for 297 years. Their greed and cruelty caused our king to seek military assistance from the Dutch. In time, the Dutch proved to be as dominating as the Portuguese. The Sinhalese called on the British to help expel them. The British made our island a crown colony in 1802 and named it Ceylon. On February 4, 1948, Sri Lanka became an independent nation. Yet today, many Portuguese, Dutch, and British businessmen remain in Sri Lanka controlling much of the finances."

I remembered again Colton's words about Sri Lanka

being the second poorest nation in the world. I could now see it for myself, and with a little better understanding.

"The women on the hillside there are Tamils, previously brought over here by the British from India to work cheaply on the plantations. They are not economically well off, nor have they ever been given Sri Lankan citizenship. The Tamils in the cities, on the other hand, are usually original inhabitants of the island. They own some of the small businesses."

I watched the women at work. It looked backbreaking as they carried their heavy burdens in the hot, humid climate, located only five degrees north of the equator.

As the van wound its way along the rugged coast on our way to the storm-stricken southern tip of the island, the scenery changed drastically. The terraced plantations became blanketed in a gray-blue mist. Violet-tipped peaks soared above the tea and spice gardens, stretching over seven thousand feet into the air.

Colton pointed to the highest mountain. "That's Adam's Peak, famous for a footprint near the summit. The Sinhalese Buddhists believe that Buddha's foot brushed the top of the mountain on his return to India after visiting Sri Lanka. The Muslims claim the footprint was made by Adam, formed when he was exiled here from the Garden of Eden. The Hindu Tamils call the mountain Samanakanda, after the brother of Rama, a Hindu god. Local Catholics claim that the footprint belongs to Saint Thomas."

"I'd like to visit the top and see the footprint for myself when we have time," I said, staring at the mysterious mountain.

But after what I would see that day—the broken houses and lives, the unforgettable look on the little girl's face when we found her in the ditch on our return—the footprint of Saint Thomas would have to wait. The tropical storm's devastation would cast an entirely new light on why I was here, making my own footprints in the dust of Sri Lanka's streets.

Chapter Three

Lallani's Compassion

Colton's home was nestled in dense jungle foliage, about two hundred yards from the road. On one side a rickety fence tried to contain the overbearing tropical growth. A driveway wound through the lush, manicured lawn leading to the white, wooden-framed house. The veranda overlooked coconut palms and bright orange bird-of-paradise blossoms. Thick rain forest blocked out what lay beyond the property line of my friend's lovely home.

Every evening of our stay after the trip to the storm-torn village, we traveled with Colton to other villages to lead Bible studies. Colton's younger sons chauffeured us to sightsee and shop during the day. Their driving kept us on the edge of our seats as they swerved in and out of the busy Colombo traffic. Horns blared. Trucks whizzed by, missing us by inches.

When we returned to the house each afternoon, we met children on their way home from school. The girls wore white dresses, many of them tattered and stained. The boys dressed in uniforms of white shorts and cotton shirts. Most of the children were barefoot.

They waved and shouted, "Hello, Hello," in English with a clear British accent. I wondered where they lived because I had not seen any other houses nearby. Every day they climbed the barbed wire fence at the edge of Colton's property. They were taking a shortcut home through his yard.

Colton told us that these children studied English in school, so I tried to talk with them. At first they were shy, and most would not speak. However, I did make friends with one little girl named Lallani who waited regularly for me every afternoon by the rickety fence. I began carrying presents of gum and candy in my pockets for her.

Lallani was a beautiful girl, thin, with dainty Caucasian features. She parted her long, black hair in the middle and drew it back in a ponytail. Bright, almond-shaped eyes accentuated her oval face and her little pug nose. Her white, ruffled dress with a torn sash was much too short for her. She looked about six, but malnutrition had stunted her growth. She was actually nine.

One day she asked, "Why don't you come to my home?"

Never having crossed the fence, I wondered what was on the other side. The dense foliage made it impossible to see beyond the barbed wire. I asked, "Where do you live?"

"Come, come see," she invited, shyly taking my hand. Lifting her over the fence, I followed her into a small village. I had not realized that this settlement existed only one hundred yards from Colton's home.

The community consisted of sixty to seventy shanties scattered at random. Each hut was approximately ten feet square, no larger than an American kitchen. Some were attached to the huts next door. Others stood alone on mounds of soil. The roofs were thatched with coconut palm branches and an occasional piece of tin. Dirt floors, baked hard as concrete, were worn smooth by many bare feet.

Sporadic trees, with trunks looking as if they had been sandpapered smooth, provided little shade from the sweltering sun; their bark had been stripped off for cooking fires. Skinny barking dogs with protruding ribs scurried in and out of the underbrush.

Children dressed in rags ran up to gain a closer look at the tall foreign visitor. Lallani still gripped my hand. She told her friends in Sinhala, "This is my friend, Uncle Deo." I discovered that the Sinhalese use the term "uncle" and "aunt" referring to older people as words of endearment.

A single water tap seemed to be the central gathering place for the women and children of the village. Some little ones lathered themselves with soap and waited their turns to rinse under the faucet. Women beat their clothes on rocks to clean them. It was hard to tell if the dirt was being forced in or out. Garments hung from thatched roofs to dry.

To my surprise, no fires burned. No food cooked. There was no refrigeration or electricity, so food usually simmered constantly on the open fires outside other shanties, but not here.

Men stood in the doorways asking with their eyes, *Who is this stranger who has come to our village?* Many adults sat around doing nothing. Since it was three o'clock in the afternoon, I asked Lallani, "Why aren't they working? Why don't I smell food cooking?"

She answered, "Nothing to do."

I persisted, "Don't they work? Don't they have jobs?"

"No work this season. Not eating," was the little girl's reply.

"Wait a minute," I gasped. "What do you mean, 'not eating?'"

Lallani's eyes sadly stared at the ground. "No food to eat. No food in the village."

"We should do something!" I exclaimed.

She looked at me in wonder, not understanding what I meant.

When we reached Lallani's home she introduced her parents. Her mother's gray hair and wrinkled face were evidence of a hard life. Her father also appeared older than his thirty-five years. Previously, he had worked for the railroad as a tinkerer, repairing wooden boxcars. But after injuring his back on the job, he was unable to work.

Lallani's six-year-old sister, Gongala, presented a total contrast to Lallani. Her circular face framed a broad smile and huge, round eyes. Gongala wore a pink checkered dress with half the buttons missing. She wore little rubber thongs, being one of the few children in the village with shoes.

Standing at the door, looking inside the tiny house, I noticed that there were no cupboards. A few worn out pots and pans hung on the wall, but I saw nothing that resembled food anywhere. I asked, "Don't you have anything to eat?"

They shook their heads.

"Can we buy food close by?" I asked.

Lallani looked surprised. Then she answered, "There's an outside market down the road. Come, Gongala and I go with you."

We hurried back to Colton's house to pick up Elaine. The four of us walked a half mile down the road to an open air market that boasted everything from bananas and rice to household goods. We stopped at a fruit and vegetable stand and viewed bins of prickly looking fruit, coconuts, papayas, seaweed greenery, and many other vegetables. After buying a sack full I asked, "What else do we need?"

"Rice," was her reply. We entered a shop with open grain sacks lying on the floor. The sides were rolled back like shirtsleeves. Brown, yellow, white oblong, flat—the rice came in all shapes and sizes.

The two girls stuck their hands into the rice to determine which to buy. They checked to see if it felt fine or coarse, because the price of the coarse grain was much lower.

Separating the rice from the chaff involved throwing it in the air. The good rice was picked out by hand. The poorer quality felt dirty and gritty because much of the chaff remained in it. That was the rice Lallani was used to buying and insisted we buy. Her eyes widened when I bought the entire sack. I slung it over my shoulder.

Elaine carried the huge bag of vegetables. Back on the street, hawkers pushed their way toward us, thrusting lace tablecloths and jewelry made of seeds in Elaine's face. Such trinkets seemed trivial compared to the value of the food Lallani's village so desperately needed.

Perspiration trickled down my forehead and neck. We edged our way down the street, weaving in and out of the people, carts, and stalls. The girls ran into an arcade filled with a dozen different stores where people bargained in Sinhala. Radios blared on six different stations; the high pitched eastern music rang in our ears.

We stopped at a fish market. Lallani pointed to a huge fish, lying on a table. Boys swung hand fans to swat the swarming flies covering the piece we considered buying. Elaine asked to be excused and went outside.

One boy held the fish in the air and asked, "How much? How much?" Bargaining with him, I bought the back half. Sri Lankans are basically vegetarians. Once Lallani's mother fried the fish with the vegetables and rice, the meal would feed many people in the village.

Rejoining Elaine, we continued down the road to a stand where we purchased backpacks for schoolbooks. Lallani pointed out some inexpensive ones, but we thought they might fall apart. Instead, we bought quality backpacks, pencils, crayons, and comb and brush sets for both girls.

Loaded down with the sack of rice, king coconuts, bags of fruit, and twenty pounds of fish, we began to trek back to the village. Elaine carried her sack of vegetables. The girls clung to their personal treasures. We looked like a three-ring circus moving down the street.

Suddenly, the girls started chattering excitedly in Sinhala to each other. I knew that the older one was trying to get the younger to ask us something, but they were too embarrassed to tell us what they wanted. Soon, we came to an open air bakery with shelves of cupcakes and loaves of bread, all crawling with bugs.

Gongala stopped and looked longingly at the baked goods. She didn't say anything, but her face left no doubt as to her desire.

"A bakery! Should we buy some bread?" I inquired. She nodded her little head. I continued, "Something else, something special? Should we buy some sweets?"

Chattering to Lallani, she pointed to a nine-inch square chocolate cake with sugary sauce smeared on the top. Normally, cake was cut into squares and sold by the piece. But I said, "No, no, we want the whole cake." The baker wrapped it in a big cardboard box and tied it with string.

Gongala's eyes widened. From her expression I assumed she had never bought a whole cake. She handed her packages to Lallani and grabbed the cake. All the way home she carried the box at arm's length in front of her, as if it contained the crown jewels of England on a satin pillow.

We wound our way along the pathway through the jungle foliage back to the girls' home. When we entered the village everyone recognized the box from the bakery. Gongala jabbered loudly that we had bought the whole cake—not just a little piece, but the whole cake! Lallani talked about the bookbags and the combs.

Their mother gasped when she saw all the food. Clapping her hands she exclaimed in broken English, "I cook food. Invite others in village, come eat." She gathered all her pots and pans and built a fire.

Lallani led us into her home. "Come Uncle Deo, Aunt Elaine, come and sit."

Although I had never entered one of the huts before, I accepted her gracious invitation and followed Elaine through the opening. A bench made of scrap lumber was located inside the doorway. Elaine cautiously sat down. The father brought out a rickety chair frame with no seat bottom, onto which I gingerly eased my massive body.

Everything the family owned could be seen from the doorway. Small straw mats used for sleeping were rolled up in a corner. Black mud walls rose to a height of about six feet. A few pieces of clothing hung on a nail protruding from the wall. The dirt floor had been swept clean, but the odor of open fire cooking hung in the air. The sparsely thatched roof gave little protection from the sun and even less from the torrential rains common to that area. A single kerosene oil lamp belched black smoke, mixing with the odors of damp earth, cooking fires, and warm bodies.

I became uncomfortable, realizing that these people lived in this situation perpetually. I felt like an intruder in spite of their hospitality.

The mother offered, "Tea, cup of tea?"

We knew we did not dare drink tea because it was not boiled. So I said, "No, no. Thank you. We wouldn't care for tea."

Our hostess wanted to serve us something to show her appreciation, so she cut into a king coconut and poured the juice in a glass jelly jar. She brought the drink to me. I looked questioningly at Elaine.

Lallani explained, "Ami only owns one glass." She called her mother Ami as many Sinhalese children did.

Then I understood that we had to share the drink. On our next shopping expedition, we would buy them a set of glasses.

Lallani and Gongala ran through the village inviting all their relatives and special friends to the feast. Meanwhile, Elaine and I returned to Colton's house, so near, and yet another world away. Looking back at the fence, the village had disappeared in the tropical undergrowth. It could all have been a dream—so different was it from the other side of the pastor's yard.

Every afternoon Lallani would wait outside the fence. She often took my hand, and we returned to her village. I wondered if perhaps I was the first white man to visit her family and friends. Sometimes, I sat and talked. On other occasions, I took Lallani and Gongala shopping.

One day while I was chatting with a group of people from the village, one of the children asked, "Where do you come from?"

"I came on a big airplane from America, across the ocean," I replied.

They watched airplanes fly overhead to the airport near Colombo, so they understood how I arrived. But they wanted to know why. "Who sent you? Why do you come to our village?"

"Jesus Christ sent me. Have any of you heard of Him?" I asked. Everyone shook their heads. No one in the village knew His name.

People in this community were all Buddhists, so I used care when talking to them about Jesus. I told them, "Jesus does not live in a temple. He is a spirit who cannot be seen. He came to earth to help people. Today His love and His Spirit dwell in His followers."

Opening a Bible story book, I showed them pictures of Jesus. I told the story of Jesus feeding the five thousand based on Luke 9:12–17. As I spoke a few words in English, Lallani translated them into Sinhala. Stories intrigued these people. They listened attentively.

I continued the story. "Late in the afternoon, the disciples came to Jesus and said, 'Send the crowd away so they can go to surrounding villages to find food, because there is nothing to eat here.'

"Jesus replied, 'You give them something to eat.'

"The disciples answered, 'We have only five loaves and two fish. How can we feed five thousand people?'

"Jesus looked up into heaven and thanked God for the bread. Then, He broke the loaves into pieces, and gave them to the disciples to pass out among the people. A strange thing happened. As the disciples broke pieces of the bread, the loaves were the same size as before. The same thing occurred with the fish. There was enough food for everyone. The village people whom Jesus fed were similar to you."

Lallani looked at me shyly and said, "And you are like Jesus. You did the same thing, Uncle Deo. You brought food to our village when we were hungry." The people nodded in silent agreement.

My throat tightened as I grasped the parallel she envisioned. I fought for words. I prayed silently, "Help me, Lord, to know what to say to these people."

I took a deep breath and stood up. Thoughts swirled in my head. "That is how I know that my God is alive. I told you He is a God of love and hope. Jesus fed five thousand. Through Him, I fed your village. Because the love of Jesus lives in me, I want all of you to know about His love, too."

During the next few days I became friends with many of these people. Lallani and Gongala often stood outside the fence by the edge of the jungle waiting for me, afternoon and night. When I saw them I stopped to chat and treat them with a piece of candy or a stick of gum from my pocket.

The day arrived when it was time to say good-bye; our "vacation" in Sri Lanka was at an end. We were not sure when, or if, we would see the girls again. We realized that Lallani and Gongala would probably live out their lives in a cycle of poverty, but we had done all we could for them while we were there.

The last evening I gave them the remaining pieces of candy and said, "Now, I must say good-bye. Remember to attend school regularly. Learn all you can."

Early the next morning I walked out on the veranda. I was surprised to see Lallani standing there. Normally she left early because she walked for an hour to reach the school.

I waved to her and she ran over to me. "Why aren't you in school?" I pleaded.

Looking at the ground, she replied, "Uncle, I took leave from school today."

"Lallani! I told you how important it is not to miss a day of school." She could tell I was upset with her. "Even though Ami and Daddy might not force you to go to school, you must attend every day. You have to get an education." Education would be the only way she could ever break the vicious cycle of poverty.

Shyly, she continued, "I'm staying home because you

are going back to America. I'll never see you again. I must stay with you to the end." I stepped toward her and placed my hands on her shoulders. I felt at a loss for words. I wanted to give her one more thing; but all my trinkets, candy, and gum were gone.

Then I reached in my shirt pocket and pulled out my worn New Testament that I always carried. Over the years, I had underlined it and written in the margins. The pages were crinkled and bent. "Lallani, I want to leave this valuable book with you. Don't let your parents sell it. It tells stories about Jesus."

Lallani nodded her head. Her lower lip quivered.

I swallowed and said, "I will pray for you, Lallani, and for Gongala and your parents, too." A lump formed in my throat. I could not speak. I felt as if I were deserting my own child.

Lallani cried softly. "Never see you again, Uncle."

I put my arms around this special little girl and held her for a moment. Then my thoughts turned to the little girl we found on the side of the road a few weeks before. I wondered how she was doing in her home, the home the pastor found for her. Maybe I was hugging her too in my heart as I held onto Lallani.

"No, no. You can't leave yet. Ami is making toffee," she exclaimed.

I thought she said coffee, and I replied, "We don't have time to drink coffee, because the plane won't wait for us. I have to leave now, honey. I'm sorry."

Elaine walked over, gave Lallani a hug, and placed a seed necklace around her neck. "They're waiting for us, Deo," she reminded me.

Again Lallani pleaded, "You must wait. Ami is making toffee."

"We have to leave now. I will pray for you daily, Lallani." I whispered, barely able to speak. Quickly I turned and walked back from the edge of the jungle not daring to look back. Once we were seated in the Volkswagen, I leaned out the window and waved to the little girl who meant so much to me.

Thoughts filled my mind as we drove away from Colton's house. What if she died after I was gone? Did she understand about Jesus? I felt utterly helpless. Yet, I could do no more at this point.

Arriving at the church, we transferred the luggage to a van. Suddenly, a runner raced up to us with a crinkled piece of paper. "Sir, Sir, this is for you!" he shouted breathlessly.

A string wrapped around the gift held a small tag that read: To Uncle Deo and Aunt Elaine. I unwrapped the package and found small, brown cubes inside that smelled like ginger and brown sugar. Several people gathered to see what the present was. "It must be a sweet of some kind," I said.

Suzanne took a piece and ate it. She exclaimed. "Ah, this is homemade toffee. Where did you get it?"

Elaine answered, "Lallani's mother must have made it for us."

Each of us ate a square of the delicious candy. Colton asked, "You don't understand what this gift really means, do you?"

"It was thoughtful of them to make us a going away present," I replied.

"No, no. You don't understand what a precious gift you are holding in your hand!" exclaimed Colton. "Sugar is the highest priced commodity in Sri Lanka. Your friends must have gathered all the rupees in the village to buy the ingredients for the toffee. The entire village won't eat for several days. That is their way of showing how much they love and appreciate you. They must have given you all that they had."

What was I willing to give in return?

Chapter Four

Home Again

Each step I took toward the ramp of the 747 jet increased my sadness. I felt that I was leaving part of myself behind on this beautiful island. Elaine and I walked slowly, wondering if we would ever return. People hurried past us. We were the last passengers to board before the door swung shut with a final clang.

When we were seated, I opened the crinkled paper and stared at the few remaining pieces of toffee. Elaine and I looked into each other's eyes, but no words could express our thoughts. I squeezed her hand to say what I could not express in words.

The stewardess stopped by my seat and asked, "Is anything wrong? Can I get you something?"

Forcing a weak smile, I shook my head. I tried to speak but words stuck in my throat. Suddenly, an urge to run off the plane and stay in Sri Lanka threatened to overcome me. Yet, in my heart, I knew that I must leave.

After what seemed an endless delay, the engines roared and the airplane taxied down the runway. As we circled the airport, I gazed out the window at the rows of coconut trees and thatched roofs. The haze of cooking smoke hung in the air. Children played in the dirt around the huts. How many of them would not see tomorrow because of malnutrition and disease? I closed my eyes and saw Lallani's face. Her words rang in my head. "You can't leave. Ami's making toffee. You can't leave, Uncle Deo." I touched the precious package in my lap.

A brief stop in Singapore for a day of shopping did little to improve my melancholy. Every child I saw on the streets reminded me of Lallani. The splendor of the bazaars and restaurants no longer attracted me. We went back to the hotel to sleep for a few hours before reboarding the airplane. Every time I closed my eyes, I saw the children of Lallani's village staring back at me. I could not get those eyes out of my mind.

The next day on the long flight home, the stewardess appeared with tray after tray of food. Looking at the huge portions, I thought, *That's enough to feed a family of four.* I tried to take a bite, but it would not go down. Emotional and physical exhaustion overwhelmed me. I could not eat.

We stopped in Detroit to spend Easter with Elaine's family. Sitting around the kitchen table, I relayed the experiences of our journey—the beauty, the devastation, the poverty, and the people. "We have returned to a blessed country of plenty. Look at the precious gift Lallani's village gave us." Reaching in my pocket, I brought out the toffee and told them the story behind it. When I had finished, everyone at the table cried.

On Sunday, we attended an Easter pageant at my sister-in-law's church. It was an extravagant affair with multi-colored costumes. What contrast to the scene in Sri Lanka! I looked at the elaborate costumes and thought of villagers without a change of clothes. So much money being spent on people who already knew Christ, when there were so many in the world who did not know Him yet! "What a waste," I whispered to myself.

A choir of fifty children dressed in white robes filled the stage. As they sang, my mind transformed the smiling, Caucasian faces into bronzed, pleading ones. Once again I saw those brown eyes, begging me to stay. The children's white robes reminded me of the tattered white dresses, shorts, and shirts of the schoolchildren I had grown to love. I looked at Elaine through misty eyes and whispered, "They're ten thousand miles away, and I still can't get away from them!"

The following week, we returned home to California. The palm trees that lined the streets reminded us of the coconut palms on the tear-shaped island so far away. Could it be that God made it into that shape on purpose? When Elaine sent me to the store, I bought the cheapest loaf of bread. I stopped entertaining business associates at expensive restaurants.

When people left food on their plates at coffee shops, I wanted to scream, "That would feed a family of ten." A tremendous change took place inside both Elaine and me. We counted every penny we spent, thinking of how many children we could feed.

As a builder I had done some repair construction on our neighbor's house before leaving for Sri Lanka. I had not charged him for my services. In return, Leo and his wife Gina took Elaine and me to dinner. We went to an exclusive restaurant in Beverly Hills, frequented by TV and movie personalities.

There were no prices on the menu. When we asked the waiter what he recommended, he announced, "Fourteen-pound lobsters were flown in four hours ago."

Leo ordered, "Lobster for everyone."

Curiously, I asked, "How much are they going for tonight?"

"Thirteen dollars a pound," was the waiter's reply.

The lobster was steamed, cut in half, and served on an enormous platter. The claw was so large, I could lay my hand inside. I looked at the white meat and was reminded of the twenty-pound fish that had fed Lallani's entire village. The lobster on my plate could have fed that village tonight. My forehead broke out in a cold sweat. Suddenly, I wanted to leave, but I was trapped. How could I explain my feelings to my dear neighbor?

Elaine stared at me. "Don't you feel well? You look pale. What's wrong?" she asked.

Blinking back tears, I tried to take a bite, but I could not. I looked at the claw and saw hundreds of tiny hands reaching up to me. I heard the sounds of the streets of Colombo—the honking horns, the high-pitched music, the chatter of children. I tried to take another bite but gave up and requested a doggy bag.

Over the next few months, we shared our Sri Lankan experiences with many of our friends. Several of them wanted to feed children as we were doing with that one little girl. We arranged sponsorships through Colton. "For the price of a cup of coffee, one child could be fed for an entire day," we explained to them.

Although I continued building houses, my enthusiasm waned. Whenever I sat down to do paperwork, my mind flashed back to all we had seen on our journey.

One day, I turned to Elaine and said, "Maybe the pressures of the business are becoming too much for me. I can't concentrate on my work. I've lost my drive."

Elaine thought for a moment, then answered, "I don't think it's stress. I think God is trying to tell you something. Maybe He's trying to whisper in your ear, but you're not listening."

Sometime during those next months, Elaine had a vivid dream. In it she was standing in the middle of a destitute village that swarmed with hungry people. Open, running sores covered their bodies. Somehow Elaine knew it was Sri Lanka, but she had never visited the exact location.

A voice directed her to go into one of the shanties. Even in her dream, she drew back, filled with horror. Realizing it was the Lord's voice, she entered into the shanty and a form, as it were, followed her inside. She found herself standing in the darkness, looking into the eyes of a woman on whom a strange light was now shining, radiating from the person beside her. She realized she was seeing a vision of Christ. His eyes fell on each person in the room. One by one they were healed, sores disappearing instantly.

In the dream, all the people in the village brought their idols and images, piled them in the middle of the streets and set them afire. Their faces lit up with the hope and serenity that Jesus brought to them. Then, the dream ended. It troubled Elaine for a few days, but she thought it was because we had talked so much about the needs of the Sri Lankan people. Soon the memory faded. A clearer understanding of the dream would come much later.

Disturbed, I visited my pastor and shared my feelings. We prayed together, and Pastor Crites asked, "Do you feel that God is calling you to do something, Deo?"

I thought back to the time, twenty years earlier, when I first became a Christian. At eighteen I wanted to attend a Bible college and become a missionary. Instead, I married and raised two children. Family obligations superseded my own desires. The timing was not right. Yet, the desire to serve God in this way never left me.

I answered, "It's strange that you would say that. Elaine said the same thing. But how do I know if it's God's will?"

He offered a suggestion. "Why don't you pray and fast to see if God reveals anything to you?"

Eighteen months before, I had built a beautiful, six-thousand-square-foot home on the top of a hill. When the recession hit, interest rates zoomed up to 21 percent, causing the bottom to fall out of the building market. The rest of my business was progressing nicely, but this white elephant had eaten up my capital for the past year and a half.

Elaine challenged me, "Set a fleece before the Lord to see if He wants you to go into full-time ministry. Give Him three days. Pray and fast for that time. The sign will be that the house sells."

I took a three-by-five index card and wrote on it, "Lord, whatever you're trying to tell me, reveal it. If you want me in full-time ministry, sell the house in three days and make an opening at the church for my ministry." I taped the index card to the mirror where I shaved. Each morning, I was reminded of my fleece.

Nothing happened on the first day. The second day,

business continued as usual, but I was not accustomed to fasting. Weak from hunger, I became a doubting Thomas. I shouted, "I should never have listened to Elaine or my pastor. I'm a builder, not a missionary. I never receive personal answers from God."

The third day, I came home early from work and wandered around the swimming pool area. Hunger made me super-sensitive to everything around me. I wanted to return to Sri Lanka; but I began to ask, "Who would provide for me if I shut my business down? Who was I to tell God to do something in three days?"

I told Elaine that I was driving to our hilltop house to check the burglar alarm for the weekend and make sure the sprinklers worked properly. My thoughts remained on my fleece. *What would God do with a builder anyway? He wanted people who graduated from Bible colleges and seminaries.*

Parking my car, I walked up the beautiful cobblestone driveway and stared at the mansion in front of me. Leaves covered the sidewalk. I grabbed the garden hose and started washing down the walkway. Minutes later, a little red sports car driven by an Oriental man pulled up and stopped in front of me. He looked unimpressive as he stepped out, wearing shorts, thongs, and a loose-fitting T-shirt.

What does this guy want? I wondered.

Coming toward me, he politely asked in broken English, "May I see house?"

"Sure, go ahead," was my unenthusiastic reply.

He took off his thongs at the door and spent thirty minutes touring the house. Returning, he said, "May I go for wife? Will you stay?"

"Do you live close by?" I wanted to know. He assured me he did, so I said, "I'll wait twenty minutes for you. Then I'm going to lock up."

Many people had walked through the home during the eighteen months it was listed on the market. Everyone wanted to buy it, but no one came up with the money. Watching him drive away, I thought, *This guy's another 'lookylou' like the hundreds who have tramped through this house before him. Dressed like that, there is no way he can afford to buy this beautiful home.*

Soon, the little red sports car returned. The wife stepped out and graciously bowed. I bowed back in the Oriental fashion. She spoke no English. They walked up to the door and removed their thongs.

After another half hour, the little man returned and said, "We like house."

"That's great," I replied, thinking *What else is new. Everybody likes the house. Everyone wants to buy the house, but who can afford it?*

The Oriental man persisted, "Who I talk to about financing?"

"You talk to me. I own the house. The price is $525,000." Excitement filled my voice. Could this man be making me an offer?

The little man looked surprised. "Oh, I thought you gardener. Five hundred twenty-five, too much," he said shaking his head.

"That's the price," was my answer. We spent several minutes bartering, and I lowered the asking price slightly.

Finally, after several offers and counter offers, he said, "I buy. Where we open escrow?"

Suddenly, the impact of the events of the past two hours hit me. I prayed silently, "No, Lord. Is this the man you sent to me? It's the third day, the eleventh hour, and the escrow office closes in ten minutes for the weekend."

Then audibly I said, "If you want to open escrow today, we'd better hurry. If we leave now, we can make it to the escrow company before they close. Follow me."

After signing the papers, I rushed home to share the news with Elaine. I found her on the patio and shouted, "Look Elaine, I have the escrow papers!"

She turned to me and said, "Do you know what that means? God gave you a miracle to show you he wants you in full-time ministry."

My face dropped, and the doubting Thomas took over

again. Maybe God didn't want me in full-time ministry. Maybe it was just a coincidence. I struggled with my thoughts for a few days, and then I went to see Pastor Crites.

He said, "Do you realize that you've experienced a miracle? I'd be afraid not to accept God's calling if I were you."

"How do I really know this is God's calling?" I asked. "How can I be sure?"

Shortly after that, Elaine became ill with pain in her right side. At the time, she taught second grade and wanted to finish the school year before doing anything about the problem. Yet, the pain persisted. Finally, she went to the doctor for tests. A sonogram revealed cysts on her ovaries that were thought to be cancerous. We were leaving on vacation for two weeks, so we decided to postpone action although the doctor recommended surgery.

The doctor became concerned when he heard our decision. That evening, I received a personal call from him. "Deo, Elaine needs to have surgery immediately. This type of cancer is fast moving, and a two-week delay could be fatal."

The next day, we sought two other doctors' opinions. Both concurred with the first surgeon. We finally agreed to take her into the hospital the next day to rerun the tests.

Before going to sleep that night, Elaine prayed, "Dear Lord, I feel called into a ministry for you. Perhaps I need a sign too. If you heal me I will resign teaching and go into this full-time work for you."

She was able to sleep, but I was not. After hours of struggling with my own thoughts, I rolled over and touched Elaine's side. Then I prayed. "Dear Lord, I know you sold the house for me; but if you really, really want me to spend my life in your ministry, heal Elaine tonight. Then I will know, beyond a shadow of a doubt, what you are trying to tell me."

The next morning, Elaine underwent another sonogram. The technician was the same person who had run the first test. He looked at the results, shook his head, and ran a second sonogram. We were waiting in the reception room when the technician came in looking puzzled and said, "The tumors that I saw a few days ago are completely gone. I've never seen this happen before!"

Elaine and I looked at each other. Then we jumped up from our chairs and hugged each other wildly. The technician's words were our answer from God.

During Elaine's childhood, she always had the dream of becoming a teacher. At the age of twenty-two with two small children at home, she returned to college to pursue this dream. For years she struggled to earn her degree without neglecting family responsibilities. Now our children were grown, and the dream was fulfilled.

So having taught for eight years, Elaine resigned from her second grade teaching position. A new dream began.

I closed my construction business, and we lived on our savings temporarily. I went into Pastor Crites's office to share my decision with him. He said, "You can have the office next to mine. I knew that God was leading you to this choice."

That night in my prayer time I thanked God for the miracles He had performed in our lives. Then I made the commitment to begin my full-time ministry.

In my mind, I could hear God guiding me to accept the challenge of this ministry. I felt a tremendous peace about my decision. I opened my Bible and read John 21:15–17: "When they had eaten breakfast, Jesus said to Simon Peter, 'Simon, son of Jonah, do you love Me more than these?' He said to Him, 'Yes, Lord; You know that I love You.' He said to him, 'Feed My lambs.'"

As the passage continued, Jesus asked Peter three times if he loved Him. He called Peter to feed His sheep. Peter was hurt because Jesus asked him three times. I was not. Now, after our third calling, I would answer, two years after our first visit to Sri Lanka.

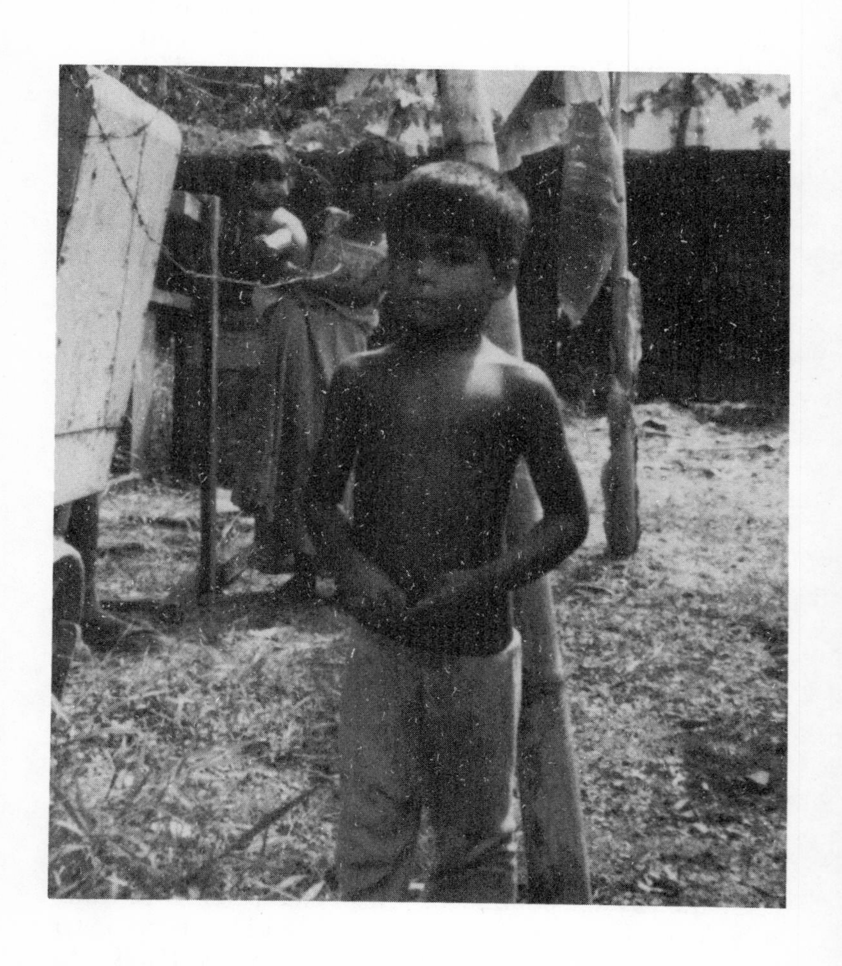

Chapter
Five

The Peanut Boy

To begin our ministry, Elaine and I spent six months in Sri Lanka. We rented a small flat which had a bedroom, a living room, and bath. The living room was sparsely furnished with a couch, two rattan chairs, and a table. Bare walls faced us on every side. Iron bars picketed the windows. We learned not to place objects on the table within arm's reach from the outside because they disappeared overnight.

Despite the revolving ceiling fans in the bedroom and living room, the temperature inside the flat remained at 120 degrees night and day. An air conditioner sat in the corner, but the cost of electricity prohibited its use except on special occasions.

The bathroom fixtures were a commode with a pull chain, a small sink, and an old-fashioned claw tub with a homemade shower hanging over it. The first night in our new home, Elaine decided to shower. Because water pressure was nearly nonexistent, cold water trickled from the outlet. Somehow, she managed to remove some of the dirt and perspiration.

When Elaine stepped from the shower, something slimy wiggled under her feet. Looking down, she screamed and retreated into the tub. Hundreds of half-inch white worms covered the red cement floor. "Deo, save me," she cried.

Rushing into the bathroom, I lifted her into my arms and carried her, dripping wet, into the bedroom. Apparently, we were the first renters for a long time. The worms lived under the tub. The moisture revived them, and they became thirsty. Half a can of Raid quenched their thirst for good.

Later that night, I woke up slapping something from my face and arms. I switched on the light. Bedbugs crawled all over Elaine and me. I ripped off the bottom sheet and discovered that the straw mattress was filled with black flecks. Jumping out of bed, we shook our only set of bedsheets. Then we emptied the remainder of the Raid can and the contents of a new one on the sheets before replacing them on the bed. With great difficulty I coaxed my wife back to a bed that now reeked with the smell of Raid.

Elaine's voice quivered as she said, "You know my greatest fear is bugs. Oh, Deo. How are we going to survive in this place?"

I did not have an answer; but I replied, "God led us to Sri Lanka. He won't give us more than we're capable of handling." I hugged her. "We're exhausted. Let's go back to bed."

Sometime later, still awake, I stared at the ceiling. Lizards seemed to play tag as they scurried back and forth. I hoped Elaine would not awaken. However, a large lizard lost its grip and fell on her face.

Startled, Elaine sat up in bed and stared at me with a bewildered look. I meekly said, "It wasn't an insect. You didn't say you were afraid of lizards. Anyway, lizards eat insects. Be thankful for them."

An icy stare told me I had better choose my words more carefully. Somehow, we managed to endure our first night without any more surprises.

On Saturday we went shopping with Colton's wife, Suzanne, at a government-owned store called Laksala, located in the heart of Colombo. Brass plates, silver, and intricate artwork were among the trinkets and handmade items available from all over Sri Lanka. Elaine wanted to buy presents to mail home for our family and friends.

Not being a shopper, I stayed outside while everyone else entered the store. I watched the steady flow of people passing by. Many stopped at the nearby corner where hundreds waited for buses. Women shaded themselves with multi-colored, tie-dyed umbrellas. Men raised handkerchiefs over their heads, attempting to hold off the blistering sun rays. Occasionally they lowered them to wipe the perspiration from their brows.

An assortment of vendors took advantage of this meeting place by setting up stalls to sell watches, shoes, water buckets, kitchen items, and new saris. Centered in the confusion, one vendor peddled peanuts from a homemade cart that looked like a barbecue on wheels. He also sold cashews and a variety of other nuts, salted or pepper-hot salted.

Like a vendor at a baseball park, he hawked his peanuts to the people who passed. "Peanuts, peanuts, hot roasted peanuts, only two rupees," he shouted above the noise of the cars, trucks, and throngs of people. When a customer approached, the vendor coiled a sheet of paper on the end of his finger to look like an ice cream cone. Folding over the sides, he poured nuts into the ready-made container.

I noticed a street urchin standing close by the vendor. He was about five years old, dressed in cut-offs and a ragged shirt, smudged with ground-in dirt. The little boy watched closely every time the vendor made a sale. As the customer walked away, the vibration of his hand caused a few peanuts to fall off the top of the cone onto the sidewalk.

The boy darted forward like a little circus monkey and retrieved the two or three fallen peanuts. Carefully dusting off each nut, he placed it in his pocket. He never ate a peanut.

I watched this scene continue for about thirty minutes. Then I walked over to the peanut vendor and asked, "Do you know that little boy?"

"What boy? Oh, that one, No, he's just a beggar," was the indifferent reply.

I knelt down and motioned with my hand for the boy to come to me. When he stood nearby, the odor of his body was overwhelming. I held my breath and asked, "Do you like peanuts?"

He nodded and I continued, "Then why aren't you eating the peanuts in your pocket?"

He put his head down and hesitated before answering, "I'm saving them for Ami and my sisters."

I looked at the vendor and said, "Give him two peanut funnels. Fill them to the brim. Make them the biggest you can."

The vendor smiled. He knew that I was doing something special for this little boy, and he wanted to play a part. He filled the funnels to the top and balanced a few extra nuts like mountain peaks on each one. "Aren't you lucky to have this nice visitor to our country buy you peanuts?" he asked.

The boy looked at me and said, "Thank you, thank you."

I took the cones and handed one to him, asking, "Can you carry these?"

A huge grin flashed on his face as he took the cone. "Sure," he answered, grabbing the top layers of nuts. He knew they would fall off when he took the first step, making him a victim to his own game. He shoved the few peanuts in the pockets of his cut-off jeans. Then he carefully did the same thing to the other funnel before grasping it in his other hand.

I put my arms around him and gave him a big hug. "When was the last time you ate?" I asked.

He shrugged his shoulders. He could not remember his last meal. Looking down at his two fists full of peanuts, he smiled at me. His eyes showed gratitude. Then he turned and walked down the street, weaving his way through the crowds.

On a sudden impulse I followed him, keeping my distance so he wouldn't see me. I shadowed him for a block before he turned down a dark alley.

At the end of the passageway, a mother and two small girls sat, huddled in a doorway. The mother's elbows rested on her knees, her chin cupped in her hands. Wisps of her dark, long hair fell forward over her cheeks framing the total despair written on her young face. She seemed oblivious to the squabbling taking place between her two toddlers. The tiniest girl was naked; the other wore a ragged dress.

Unobserved, I snapped a picture of them. The boy ran to his mother, lifting his funnels of peanuts high in the air. She spread the skirt of her sari to form a place to drop the nuts. He poured the contents of the cones into her lap and emptied his bulging pockets. He jabbered on and on, pointing down the street in my direction and gesturing with his hands. Still, he did not notice me.

His mother found a sheet of newspaper and quartered it to use as placemats. Doling out the precious peanuts according to the size of the person, she gave herself the most, the boy the second largest portion, and so on. The family formed a circle around her as she handed each their placemat. The feast began.

I walked up to them. The boy smiled. He explained to his mother in Sinhala, "He bought the peanuts. This is the man."

The mother spoke no English but communicated her gratitude with her eyes. The family's meager personal belongings lay on the doorstep, indicating that the end of this dark alley was the place they called home.

The family finished their treat in a matter of minutes. Not one peanut fell to the ground. Not one crumb or peanut skin remained.

I reached in my pocket and located a hundred rupee note, the equivalent of a week's pay. I handed it to the mother saying, "God loves you, and I love you too. I wish there was somewhere to take you." Yet I knew that Sri

Lanka provided no welfare programs for abandoned children and wives.

The young woman looked at the money, and her face beamed. I held my hand out to shake her hand, but she clasped mine in hers and kissed it.

I said, "No, no, you don't have to do that," but she didn't comprehend.

She put one hand on her mouth and patted her children's heads with the other as if to say, "This will feed them."

I nodded my head to show her I understood. Even though a tremendous language barrier existed between us, our eye contact provided a strong bond.

She bowed her head, saying thank you in the Sri Lankan manner. I patted each child on the head before I turned and walked down the alley.

Just as I reached the front of Laksala's store, Elaine and Suzanne emerged. My wife said, "How can you stand out here in the heat doing nothing? Wait until you see the elegant brass plates and woven placemats I purchased."

I could not reply. Little did she know what had occurred. On the way back to our flat, I sat quietly in the van. With every passing doorstep, I became aware of the hundreds of families who barely survived, living in the doorways of Colombo.

Later Elaine inquired, "It's not like you to be so quiet. What's wrong?"

I told my wife and Suzanne the story of the peanut boy and his family.

Suzanne said, "Deo, my lifelong dream has been to give new hope to abandoned mothers and their children. I want to teach them skills, so they can care for themselves and their families. It's a responsibility our church is willing to accept, if we can find enough funds."

I thought of the busy people on the Colombo streets. No one stopped to help the families huddled on the doorsteps and the beggar children scrambling for peanuts. Overwhelmed by hunger, the poor wandered aimlessly through the streets. Many were too weak to struggle but too tough to die easily. They cried for help, but no one listened.

That night, I knelt and prayed, "Lord, keep me sensitive to the needs of these people. Don't let me become hardened to the concerns of those around me. I can't help everybody, but I can help some. Teach me to keep my eyes open every day, everywhere I go. In Jesus' name, Amen."

Once again, I knew my purpose in Sri Lanka. Through a little peanut boy, God revealed His divine plan for our work halfway around the world from our home.

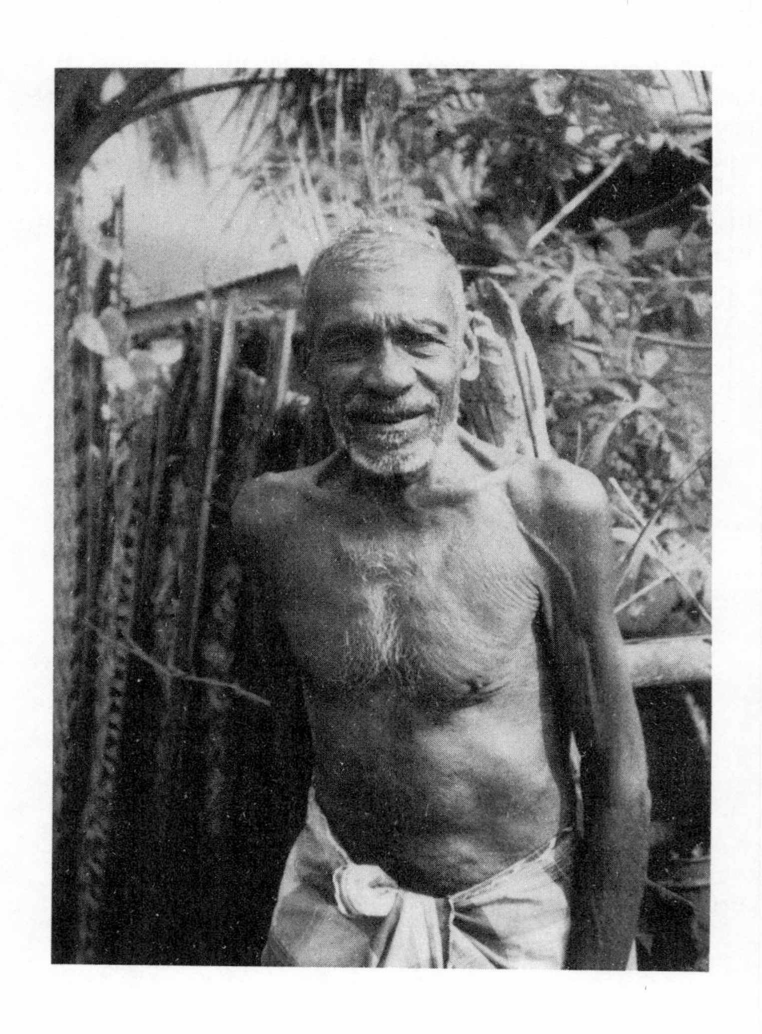

Chapter Six

Prem, The Dignified Hindu

Many mornings the smell of incense and high-pitched chanting awakened us. A cinder block in the wall over the bed acted as a draw, pulling the smoke and noise into our bedroom. Our flat adjoined the house of our landlord Prem, a delightful man, and his wife. We often wondered what went on in their home at such an early hour, but we never asked.

Often in the evenings, our landlord's wife, Raksha, invited us to join them for coconut milk or fresh pineapple drinks. A petite and well-groomed lady, Raksha pulled her gray hair back into a large bun. In this foreign land, her gracious smile made us feel welcome. She seemed active and spry for her age, which we guessed to be about seventy. Although her household servants kept the house immaculate, she was constantly wiping tables, dusting furniture, and rearranging knicknacks.

Prem always wore a white shirt and sarong. Crippled by arthritis, he was stooped and walked with a cane. The dignified Hindu was short and balding. He wore thick, black, horn-rimmed glasses dating from the fifties. Yet, Prem carried an air of distinction and well represented the elite Brahman class to which he belonged.

Each morning Prem waited with us on the veranda for

our driver, who was always late. One day he said, "I'm Hindu by birth, but I've attended Colton's church where I heard about Jesus Christ. Come into my dining room and see my altar."

Elaine and I followed him into the dining room. The olive-green wall that housed his altar backed to one wall of our bedroom. Now we knew the answer to those strange, early morning chants. Elaine and I glanced at each other and smiled.

The altar was a giant structure standing in the corner containing over a hundred Hindu gods on the many different levels of shelves. Nestled among the flickering candles and burning incense was a statue of Mary, the mother of Jesus.

Being a wealthy man, Prem was able to purchase many expensive idols. His favorite was a brass Ganesha, the elephant-head god. A large, bronze Buddha sat in the center. The Dancing Siva was carved out of teak, as was the dark goddess Kali, who held a bowl of blood.

When we returned to the veranda, Prem asked, "Who is Jesus? Where did He come from? Can you help me find the true meaning of life?" Prem was searching for fulfillment in life—something his hundred gods had not provided for him.

In the middle of these profound questions, our driver arrived. Elaine looked at the elderly man and said, "We don't have time to answer your questions now, but I do want to pray with you. We will talk later."

She prayed, "Dear God. Bless Prem, his wife Raksha, and their house. Please open their hearts to your Word. In Jesus' name, Amen."

The next morning, the dignified Hindu greeted us with more questions. We tried to explain about Jesus in a few sentences, but Prem did not understand. Elaine suggested, "Why don't we have a Bible study each morning before our driver arrives? Then I can teach you about Jesus. Shall we begin tomorrow?"

Prem agreed. Promptly at 8:30 AM the following day

we heard the tapping of the metal-tipped cane. With a Bible clutched under his arm, this learned man of distinction became a student once more.

Surprised I asked, "Where did you get the Bible?"

"Someone came to my door many years ago and handed this book to me, but he never returned to explain it. I have read the Bible and know it contains much knowledge, but I don't understand its meaning. Please help me."

Elaine began with the Gospel of John. They read the first chapter together, and she assigned Prem the second chapter for homework. He returned each day with notes he had taken and thoughtful, written questions. This seventy-year-old man who had lived all his life in a pagan land voiced hunger for the gospel. God gave Elaine many insights to present the meaning at his level.

The morning study continued for several weeks. As time passed, Prem began to realize that there is only one God. One day he stated, "I need to know who Jesus Christ is in my own life. I'm ready to serve one God."

"You can't go back to the altar in your dining room and call upon those other gods," my wife warned. "Once you accept Jesus into your heart, you can never again depend on any other gods."

The elderly man continued, "You have a power that I can feel. None of the other gods provides that power. Pray with me."

The three of us knelt in prayer. Afterwards, Prem said, "Now I can feel that power within me."

Prem continued to come to our house every morning. His face looked radiant. He walked faster, as if his arthritis was getting better even as his spiritual health improved. After a seventy-year search, he had finally found meaning in his life. He seemed more at peace within himself.

While Elaine and Prem held their Bible studies every morning, I busied myself with the paperwork of setting up our ministry. Colton and Suzanne had introduced us to many Christian pastors in the area. I asked them if they were interested in establishing feeding centers in the churches. I studied their culture to avoid overstepping boundaries and offending them.

Seven pastors responded favorably, and Elaine and I went to work. These men knew the families in their villages who most needed food. We began our feeding centers with the children of these families, giving us the opportunity to share the gospel with the poorest of the poor.

By the end of six months, we were feeding eighty children daily in the seven centers. A different local church sponsored each center, all located within a forty-mile radius of Colombo. However, the financial assistance came from America. Elaine and I personally sponsored ten to fifteen of the children. Our church in California and other friends provided the remaining contributions. At this point, we had not branched out to other churches and communities for our monetary contributions. The numbers fed seemed large, but since basic food was so cheap, we were able to feed a child well for a fraction of what it would have cost us in America.

Each morning we met with the different feeding center leaders. We educated them, exchanging ideas that blended western methods with eastern culture.

Traveling to one of our feeding centers often became a day-long project. The feeding center at Chowlow was approximately forty miles from Colombo, but the journey took four or five hours by winding road. By the time we met with the leaders for a couple of hours and returned, twelve hours had elapsed. On the way home, we usually bought vegetables and fresh fruit.

One evening we saw men butchering a cow along the side of the road. Normally the beef hung from string stretched between bamboo posts until sold. The length of time ranged from a matter of days to weeks. Because of the swarming flies and lack of refrigeration, the beef usually was unsafe to eat. However, I knew this meat was fresh. Only one can of American spaghetti sauce remained in our cupboard. How good it would taste with fresh beef! I bartered with the butcher until he reduced the price to twenty-five cents a pound. I purchased four pounds.

When we reached home, Elaine bolted the meat grinder to the corner of the table. I turned the crank, but the meat grinder locked up. I took it apart, cleaned it, and inserted more meat. Again, the grinder jammed.

My mouth watered for the spaghetti and meat sauce which would be our last meal with American ingredients. I used our sharpest knife and sawed on the beef for an hour and a half, cutting it into small pieces. Finally, I realized that the meat was so tough that even tiny pieces would not go through the blades of the grinder.

Elaine fried the fillet slices in the skillet with onions. We sat down to relax for a few minutes. Suddenly, a strange odor filled the air. I asked, "What can that be? It smells terrible."

"Maybe the onions weren't fresh," answered Elaine. She stirred the meat and onions into the spaghetti sauce. Soon the meal was cooked and we sat down to our feast. After saying the blessing, I took a bite. Seconds later, I raced to the bathroom and spit the food into the sink, wondering what that cow had eaten. I never tasted anything worse.

When our driver arrived to take us to a church meeting, I asked, "Would you care for some spaghetti?"

"Don't mind." He seated himself at the table. He took a bite and said, "Ummmmm! This is delicious!"

For several days, we fed spaghetti to anyone who came to our door. They all agreed with our driver that the "American" spaghetti was delicious. We never again bought fresh beef in Sri Lanka!

Each day was a challenge. We arose at sunrise to the chattering of birds outside our window and the smell of burning incense. The heat became intense by six o'clock.

Our mornings began with the chore of boiling water for coffee. However, this process actually started the night before when we tied a towel over the faucet to serve as a filtering system while we poured the water into jugs. Then the water was boiled for twenty minutes to purify it.

Much residue still remained in suspension, so the next step was to pour the water through a commercial filter. Seven hours later, one gallon of purified water remained to be used for our morning coffee and drinking water. Our filter clogged constantly, requiring me to dismantle and clean it every time it was used.

Every morning we bought bread from a boy who came by with thirty to forty loaves tied to the back of his bicycle. The loaves tasted fresh and delicious, but we had to watch for small stones or beetles when we sliced them. Peanut butter and jelly on bread, coffee, and fresh fruit served as our usual breakfast menu.

Normally we left our apartment by nine and returned by six in the evening. Since there was no kitchen in our apartment, Elaine cooked our dinner on the bathroom floor with a one-burner stove. Exhausted, we fell into bed every night by 8:30 PM unless we had a church meeting. Sometimes, frustrated by the heat, we held our meetings in the air-conditioned lobbies of the large hotels in downtown Colombo.

One day while carrying the garbage outside, I noticed a woman sitting next to our trash can. Often beggars gathered around the bin, fighting over empty jars and cans. They used these castoffs for storing flour, spices, and other staples to prevent ants from eating them. I glanced at the young woman and noticed that she held a newspaper in her arms.

After Elaine finished her Bible study with Prem, she decided to go to the church to check for our mail. We found mail service to be more reliable if mail was addressed to Colton's church. Elaine began walking the few blocks to the church.

The woman, still clutching the newspaper, stood up and followed her. The young woman's matted hair fell in clumps around her thin, oval face. She was dressed in rags. Her beautiful, dark piercing eyes stared at Elaine. She begged, "Rupees, rupees."

Elaine did not want to give her rupees, knowing the

young woman would be there every day to beg at our gate. Elaine shook her head and kept walking down the dirt road.

The young woman put her hand on her mouth indicating hunger. She continued embracing the bundle of newspaper in her arms. Elaine assumed that she had picked up cans, potato peelings, and metal from our trash can.

Because theft is widespread, many private roads terminate at massive iron gates. The wealthy Buddhist who lived in the large house at the end of our street owned the gate. I explained to him that I worked at the church on the other side of his property. He granted us permission to use his gate. Walking around his property required a three block walk.

The gatekeeper beamed a smile at Elaine as she approached. We always took a piece of candy or gum to give the young man who carefully guarded his master's property. Elaine handed him a candy bar. The gate swung open.

The woman continued to follow Elaine. But as the iron gate began to close, she realized that she would not be allowed past the gatekeeper. She unwrapped the newspaper to reveal a newborn baby.

Shuddering, Elaine stared at the naked child. The mother was so thin that she could not provide milk for her infant. Elaine dug into her purse and located some money. She handed several rupees through the gate to the young mother.

The young woman smiled. She alternately pointed to the child and to her own mouth, indicating that she would use the money to feed the starving baby.

Elaine's heart was touched. She thought, *How could I not give to this woman?* There were so many beggars; we could not feed them all. It would have been easy to say, "I've given so much already! I can't give any more."

In tears, Elaine returned to the flat. She told me about the young mother and child. I was reminded of another child, born in a stable many years before. I wondered how swaddling clothes might have differed from newspaper.

How much could a family carry on a donkey to use for a newborn's clothing? I thought of the Christ child, who also came unnoticed by those in Bethlehem.

Normally, if a person gives to the destitute, a beggar will return again and again. Mysteriously, we never saw the woman again. Was she an angel in disguise, sent to open our hearts and once again remind us of our purpose?

Chapter Seven

Soma's Fishing Village

On our first visit to Sri Lanka, Colton introduced us to Jerry and Anita, a delightful couple who became our close friends. Jerry grew up on a farm in Nebraska and met Anita at the college they both attended. They fell in love, married, and returned to her home country of Sri Lanka to live. Not only did Elaine and I enjoy their company, but we relished the opportunity to speak American slang and escape from the proper British dialect common to Sri Lanka.

One night while we were eating dinner at their home, Jerry said, "I want to take the gospel to a fishing village nearby. It's a large community of about ten thousand people, where deep roots of Buddhism go back generations. I'm not sure how to begin because of the strong Buddhist control. However, I'm willing to try."

"Sounds good," I agreed. "Why don't you?"

"I want you to come with me, Deo."

I wanted to help my friend, but establishing the feeding centers had turned into a six-day-a-week job. "I'd like to go Jerry, but I honestly don't know when I can find the time."

Several days later, Jerry knocked on the door of our flat. "I've been talking to the people in the fishing village. One lady named Soma wants us to share the gospel with her friends. I told her we'd return this evening. Please come with me, Deo. I need your support."

Exhausted from working fourteen-hour days, I wanted to say no. Yet, when I looked into Jerry's pleading eyes, I knew I could not refuse. "Let's go," I said.

Jerry's Volkswagen bug crept through Colombo's snarled traffic. Finally, we were out of the city and traveling along the coast toward the fishing village. Thirty or forty minutes later, we turned onto a dirt road. The road ended near a beach where we parked the car and began walking.

We checked the point where we would leave the beach and return to the car. There were no lights or signs. We could not chance losing our way on this deserted stretch of beach.

As we hiked along the ocean, crystal-clear water billowed into tiny, white caps and broke on the shore. The sun, framed by monsoon clouds, glowed red on the horizon. Golden streaks crisscrossed the sky and reached into the shimmering water. Sky and water blended to form a glorious sunset.

Generations of fishermen had depended on the ocean for their livelihood. Rugged logs, hewn out on the inside and lashed together with rope woven from coconut husks, formed rough fishing canoes. They were lined up on the beach in a row, their noses pointing out to sea. Outriggers extended from the sides to keep the boats from turning over during rough seas.

One fisherman's lone dugout bobbed like a cork on the water near us. He shouted at the teenager with him to haul in the nets. They labored together to wrestle the gear aboard. Three or four small fish dropped into the bottom of the boat.

I shook my head. "Not much for a long day's labor, is it?" I asked Jerry.

He replied, "They are lucky. At least their family will eat tonight."

We continued walking. Soon the village came into view. I shivered as a light mist began to fall. The stench of fish hung in the air. The walls of one hut connected to the adjoining one. Hundreds of shanties tied together formed a bizarre maze. I could not tell where one home ended and another began.

Piles of dry palm fronds formed the roofing. Because of the heavy rainfall, these roofs lasted only six to eight months. After that time, more thatchings were stacked on top to keep out the torrential rains. If one spark from a cooking fire ever caught, the entire community would go up in smoke.

When we arrived at the village, hundreds of small children scampered out of the huts to greet us. Recognizing us as foreigners, they wanted to sell us their handmade trinkets, beads, and woven bags.

Jerry asked, "Where is the home of Soma?"

One little boy said, "Come with me. Come."

The other children followed behind us, jabbering in Sinhala. Bloated stomachs and ginger-colored hair showed the trademarks of malnutrition. Rat and insect bites covered their legs, often resulting in running sores.

Because there were no doors or windows, we looked directly into the opening of each hut. Small fires burned in the center of some—those who would be lucky enough to eat that night. Tough-looking fishermen and women stood by the doorways of their huts, silently staring at the intruders.

I remembered the stories of people entering fishing villages such as these and never returning to Colombo. A chill went up my spine. I prayed, "Dear Lord, please keep Jerry and me safe tonight."

We wound our way into the village for nearly half a mile. Darkness descended. The mist changed to a steady, soaking rain. Slippery mud covered the winding pathways and alleys that intertwined between the shanties. Footing became treacherous, but at least the rain flushed out the black channels of the open sewers.

Finally our young guide stopped in front of a shanty and grinned. Jerry asked him, "Is this the home of Soma?"

He nodded. A petite lady stepped through the doorway. Two little girls and a young boy stood behind her. The smallest girl bashfully placed two fingers in her mouth and bowed her head. The other girl clung to her mother's skirt.

Jerry stepped forward and said, "Hello, Soma. This is my friend, Deo. He is interested in children and in Jesus, too."

She smiled at me and nodded. "I told my neighbors about this Jesus, whom you mentioned, who was a fisherman. My friends want to meet you tonight and hear your stories. But first, I cook you a meal."

We followed her into the hut and learned about her husband. Few fishermen owned boats. Most, like her husband, daily waded out in the surf with a hook and a fishing line. Her husband always carried a little bit of bait in his pocket while wading on the coral reef. Since this was not the season for fish, he usually caught only a few small ones to feed his family, although he would spend twelve to fourteen hours fishing. Tonight, he had not yet returned.

Sometimes, the fishermen borrowed money from a lender in the village who wanted half of the next season's catch in return. The price was high, so Soma's family tried to exist on the fish her husband brought home.

In the eight-foot square hut, all the family's possessions were visible. Her husband's one shirt hung on a nail in the corner. The children owned only the clothes they wore. Three empty tin cans and a couple of stained jars sat on a wooden plank. Crude iron pots hung over them.

Soma placed twigs for a small fire in the center of her floor and lit them. She took her last bit of rice, approximately a half cup, and dumped it into a pot of water. Running her fingers along the sides of the container, she made sure every grain came out. Then she took two small potatoes, sliced them, and placed them in the pot. She cut up several thumb-sized carrots and added the curry and other spices to prepare the meal.

Glancing around the shanty, I realized that this meal contained all the remaining food in the house. Her vegetable and rice containers stood empty. I looked at the tiny woman and asked, "When did you last eat, Soma?"

She counted backwards on her fingers and replied, "Three days ago."

I turned to Jerry and spoke fast so Soma could not understand. "I can't eat the woman's last meal. The children watch every move their mother makes. They're hungry."

The room filled with smoke from the fire, hiding the tears that formed in my eyes. The odor of curry permeated the air as the pot boiled. "Jerry, I can't eat the family's last meal," I persisted.

Jerry frowned. "We must. She'll be offended if we don't accept her hospitality. We'll have to trust God to provide for her."

I thought of Elijah and the widow of Zarephath in 1 Kings 17. She baked Elijah a cake of bread with her last oil and flour. Elijah knew that God would replenish it, but I hadn't any revelation from God that He would do it for her. I could not let Soma and her children starve.

Soma located the dirty rag that she used for her cleaning. She dusted the tops of her two broken saucers. Then she carefully dipped half the meal in one saucer for Jerry and half in the other for me.

What could I do? The children's eyes stared at me as if to say, "Are you going to eat our last grain of rice?" Pleadingly, I looked at Jerry.

"We have no choice," he answered sadly.

I finally took a bite and tried to swallow it. Suddenly, I thought of a solution. "This is a wonderful meal you have cooked," I said. "It has nice flavor. But you know, Soma, I just ate another meal before I came. If I eat this, it will be too much for me. Would you be offended if I gave my plate to your children?"

She looked at me and shook her head. Jerry and I set the saucers on the floor. The children attacked the plates like wild dogs that had not eaten in weeks. In a matter of moments, the half cups of rice vanished.

Once again, I turned to our petite hostess and said, "Soma, I appreciate your willingness to serve us. I'd like to pray with you, asking God to especially bless your family and your house."

A delightful smile flashed on the tiny lady's face. Jerry offered the prayer. When everyone shut their eyes, I reached in my pocket and pulled out a fifty rupee note, worth about two dollars. Bending down and making sure no one was watching, I lifted one of the cracked saucers and slipped the money underneath.

When the prayer ended Soma said, "I must find my neighbors." She bowed and rushed out of the hut. We followed her outside where we were greeted by eight or nine of her friends.

Soma returned with more people. "I told them about the fisherman who helped people catch fish. I told them you would tell the story of your Jesus."

Waves of compassion overwhelmed me as I stood by Soma's doorway and stared at the hundreds of people arriving. The rain had stopped. Some villagers sat on the damp ground, others stood. I began speaking. "Jesus came to a fishing village along the shores of Galilee. That village was similar to yours. He loved those fishermen, and He loves you. He taught the people while standing in one of the fishing boats. When He finished speaking, He said to Peter, 'Go into the deep water and put the nets down for a catch.'

"Peter answered, 'Master, we have worked hard all night and haven't caught anything. But because you ask, I will try again.'

"This time, the fishermen caught so many fish that their nets began to break. A shout for help signaled their partners in another boat to assist them. Soon, both boats overflowed with fish. They began to sink.

"When Peter saw this, he fell at Jesus' feet. His partners,

James and John, were astounded at the catch of fish they had captured.

"Jesus told them not to be afraid. They pulled their boats on shore, followed Him, and became His disciples. This story is told in Luke 5:1–11 in the Bible, a book about Jesus."

While I spoke, mothers nursed their babies. Children walked up and touched my light skin as if it carried a magical power to cure their hunger and suffering. For a moment, I seemed to absorb the feeling of the fishermen and their families.

"I can't feed you rice and fish like Jesus did, but I can feed your souls. Just as Jesus loved those fishermen, He loves you. Jerry and I love you, too."

The faces of the rough fishermen softened. They listened intently to every word. When I finished, they asked, "How can I learn more about your Jesus? How do I find food for my soul?"

Jerry answered, "Jesus sent us to help you. I know this is the first time many of you have heard of Him. Tomorrow, I hope to open a building down the road. Someone will be there to pray with you, share your concerns, and answer your questions. Now, I'd like to thank Soma who brought the good news of Jesus Christ to you. And I'd like to thank all of you for allowing us to visit your village and for listening to us."

Each man stepped forward and shook Jerry's hand. Then, they each shook mine. Some held the grip and stared at me as if to say, "Remember me." A young man brought Jerry and me each a green, syrupy drink. The people had taken up an offering to buy these for us. I took a small sip and handed the rest to the small children congregating around my feet. I knew I would never forget these people.

I stared at the group of tough fishermen one last time, remembering the stories of visitors to fishing villages such as this who never returned to Colombo. Yet, I knew that

God had touched many hearts tonight. We had nothing to fear.

We hugged Soma and followed the children, retracing our steps through the winding streets. Flickering oil lanterns and candle flames cast eerie shadows on the walls of the shanties.

The children left us on the beach. The black shapes of pillar-like palms paralleled the moonlit path, guiding us back to Jerry's car. As we walked along the beach, we watched each step. Without sanitation facilities, the people often used the beach as their restroom hoping the waste would wash out to sea.

Soon we were back to where Jerry had parked the car. It was very late when we arrived back in Colombo that night.

The next day, Jerry located a shack nearby, suitable to use as a church. The owner rented him the three rooms inexpensively. That night, fifteen people arrived for prayer and more stories of Jesus.

In time, many came to be blessed in this church. Mothers seeking medical assistance brought their sick children. Jerry provided medicine for common diseases, scratches, burns, and rat bites. He offered soup and bread for the children.

Today, he feeds hundreds of children daily. Every night, approximately one hundred and fifty people gather at his church for prayer and worship. This center is not under our direct control, but we help financially. When Jerry opened a training center, he dedicated the building to Elaine and me.

Through one woman's caring, her village now has a church, a feeding center, and a vocational training program. Soma's spiritual hunger overrode her physical hunger. I will always remember the expression on her face when she offered us her last meal.

Soma currently works at the feeding center. Her family has food each day and clothing to wear. God used her as

His instrument in a chain of blessings. She is a Christian, a living testimony to her village. She brings many people into the feeding center and to the church. God's work on earth is accomplished through individuals. It reminded me that, just as our ministry started with one little girl, Jerry's church had begun with one woman named Soma.

Chapter Eight

Hell's Seventeen Acres

One afternoon, soon after my visit to the fishing village, I hurried along a pathway following a young guide to a new destination on the outskirts of Colombo. Brushing a wisp of hair from her wet forehead, Elaine rushed to catch up with me. Her thin summer dress dripped with perspiration. When she reached my side, I placed my arm around her waist. We walked on, following our teenage leader through the pathways that wound their way between tin-roofed shanties.

Oxcarts loaded with firewood bumped along the pot-holed road. Shrewd men and women sold their coconuts, bruised bananas, and pineapples from flimsy tables and stalls along the edges of the pathway. Toothless aged women, miniskirted prostitutes, and homeless children filled the streets, jostling elbows with each other. A few customers stopped to finger the fruit and barter, then moved on. Bleary-eyed men invited us into their dimly lit tea shops.

The combined smells of rotting garbage, burning fire-wood, and curry hung like a suffocating blanket in the heavy air. Elaine stopped, saying she was nauseated. We waited while she regained her composure

"Come, almost there," our guide said in his broken English.

We continued to follow him, unsure of our exact destination. Entering a narrow alley, people with hollow eyes and consumptive coughs were scattered everywhere. Some slept. Others pulled their malnourished bodies and twisted limbs toward the unexpected guests pleading, "Rupees, rupees for the poor." We carefully avoided stepping on a hand or foot.

A young woman squatted next to a broken sewer pipe in the gutter. She filled a battered cooking pot with putrid water. Nearby, an old man scooped water from the same gutter and poured it over his body for a bath. Several naked children splashed and played in the stream of runoff.

Surely, this is the place he wants us to see, I thought. Yet, the young guide walked on and climbed through a hole in the wall. On the other side, people clustered around one of the fetid ponds, a dead end for the garbage and sewage that flowed down the open trenches. In contrast, green lily pads thrived on the natural fertilizer.

The guide led us through another hole in the wall and stopped. Here we were surrounded by small huts, thrown up in a haphazard fashion. Bits of wood that had washed ashore from the Indian Ocean were held together by sticky, gray mud. A fifty-gallon drum, split down the middle and flattened into walls, formed one home. Another was composed of bits of tin and slabs from a wooden crate.

The boy shouted in Sinhala, and eight or nine people streamed from each shanty, running to greet us. "Welcome to Hell's Seventeen Acres," our young guide said with a bow.

Hell's Seventeen Acres, located near the garbage dump, has to be the poorest area of Colombo. Eight thousand people are crammed into an area no larger than a city block. Six thousand of them are children. Most never go to school but spend their days foraging through the garbage dump for pieces of tin, scraps of paper, or slivers of food. Cow dung is used to slicken the floors to make them water resistant. Diseases breed in the manure, often resulting in death because there are no medicines readily available.

Despair leads fathers to sell their daughters into prostitution. Rats outnumber people drastically. Thieves steal a man's only blanket for one more glass of the cheap, local liquor. Killings with axes, hoes, and knives occur daily, making the crime rate in this section the highest in Sri Lanka. Each smaller community in this man-made jungle is controlled by a local dictator, meting out mafia-type justice.

This area evolved from the Sri Lankan government's decision to widen the highway from the airport to the downtown government buildings in Colombo. Clearing the road meant uprooting thousands of families and bulldozing their shanties. Herding these people into a few acres created a prison without walls known as Hell's Seventeen Acres.

Some of these people found jobs at the docks unloading fishing boats or at the fish houses. Others performed odd jobs such as hauling loads on two-wheel carts. No automobiles can reach the center of this area, and most of the inhabitants suffer from hunger and unemployment. They consider themselves fortunate if they eat one meal every three days.

Most of the people in this area are Buddhists. Each shanty contains a household god to protect that home. Many of the children, although scantily dressed, wear many bracelets on their arms, placed there by the local Buddhist priests to ward off evil spirits.

One day Suzanne confided to us that she hoped to place a feeding program, and ultimately a church, in this distressed area. One of her relatives owned a small lot that could be purchased for a reasonable price. We had come to see the land.

A woman who knew the location of the lot took us there. Several coconut trees stood in one corner. A squatter had lived on the property for twenty-five years. He claimed the coconuts and the shade of the trees. Several other families lived in shanties on the fringes of the land.

Clothes hung from the branches of palm trees, drying in the sun.

As Elaine surveyed the scene, the color drained from her face. "Deo, this is the area I saw in my dream. Remember that dream I had before we returned to Sri Lanka?" she whispered.

It was a dream about this destitute village, filled with row after row of sad-faced people. She remembered how Jesus had entered the houses in the dream, teaching and healing, telling the people to collect their household gods and to set them on fire.

Standing in what seemed like the same spot, Elaine relived her dream. I looked at her and said, "How can we build a feeding center here? The needs are overpowering."

"But, Deo, the dream. The Lord showed me what was going to happen here."

A group of children followed us on our tour of the area. I reached in my pocket for a sack of candy. There seemed to be enough for everyone, so I did not anticipate any problems. I handed one piece to each child.

Suddenly, several larger boys jumped on top of the smaller children and knocked them to the ground, stealing their candy. The younger ones did not cry. Many showed battle scars from previous scuffles of that sort. All were pocked with rat bites and open sores on their faces, arms, and legs. While I watched the rule of survival of the strongest in action, chills crept up my spine.

Later, we retraced our steps through the winding pathways, through the hole in the fence, and back to a place where we caught a bus.

"This is a challenge beyond anything we've ever seen," I said. "Where do we begin? There are thousands of boys and girls living there like the ones who fought over the candy."

My wife smiled and replied, "We start with one, remember?"

I thought again of the little girl I had found by the side of the road. Then I thought of Lallani and her toffee, the peanut boy, and all the others. I recounted the work involved in setting up our first feeding center. I knew that Elaine was right. God would provide a plan. Here again, we would start with one—with what we had.

The next week, we returned to America to raise more funds for the feeding centers. I told congregation after congregation about our experience in Hell's Seventeen Acres. I mentioned it also to a friend who was a building contractor. He seemed concerned, but said nothing more about it. I did not pursue the subject with him further.

Several months later, Suzanne and Colton came to California. While traveling together in my car, Suzanne said, "We still want to purchase the piece of property in Hell's Seventeen Acres. It will cost $2,200. Do you know where we can obtain the funds, Deo?"

I knew that neither of us could afford the extra money. I suggested, "Why don't we trust God to provide for us in the church service tonight if He wants us to go ahead with building plans there."

When they did not answer, I glanced in my rearview mirror. The back seat of my large Oldsmobile engulfed the tiny Sri Lankan minister and his wife. I prayed silently, "We are small, and our need is great. Help us, Lord."

Colton preached an eloquent message at our church that evening. When he finished his sermon, Suzanne sang and said, "There's an urgency near Colombo that I'm afraid to put my hand to. The need is so great. Please pray with me on this matter."

She had not mentioned the exact need, but my contractor friend whom I had spoken to earlier stepped forward and handed them a check for $2,200. After the service Suzanne said, "It's a sign from God to purchase the lot. We don't have two bricks to put together yet, but I'm going to buy that land!"

I looked at Suzanne and asked, "What do you think a church would cost?"

"Approximately $15,000," she replied.

Two months later, Colton mailed drawings for the proposed new church to us. I looked at them and knew that I was seeing a $200,000 structure. "We can never afford that!" was my reaction.

I shipped the drawings back with a letter of concern. Soon, we received a delightful reply from Suzanne telling us not to worry. The building could be constructed in stages, and the first stage would cost only $15,000. This would be the feeding portion of the building.

Maybe we were narrow-minded. As the money was raised, we could build the remainder. Suzanne's faith inspired us.

The leader appointed to run the center was Suzanne's sister, Birdie, whom we nicknamed Sister Birdie. A friendly woman with lots of charm and a beaming smile, her gray hair was pulled back in a tight bun. Large, dark-rimmed glasses rested halfway down the bridge of her nose. She was stoutly built and spoke with authority. Her brown eyes shone with an intensity not yet dimmed by age. She walked into Hell's Seventeen Acres, assessed the situation, and went to work. In talking to the people, she determined the most desperate family situations. Her stern regimentation was backed up with love and compassion.

Reaching Hell's Seventeen Acres required several bus transfers and a long walk. The buses never ran on schedule, and hour-long waits were not uncommon. However, this sixty-year-old woman showed a tremendous amount of energy. Sister Birdie never seemed to tire while carrying out this overwhelming task.

Several years before, a church program was conducted briefly in a private home in this area, but the director never gained command of the children. During the Bible study, they would excuse themselves to go to the restroom. While they were out of the room, they stole everything in the building that was not bolted down. One time they lifted the bathroom sink out of the window. In exasperation, the director gave up and left. Now all that remained was a gutted-out structure with broken windows.

Sister Birdie decided that the children who took part in

this earlier program would be the ones to approach, since they had had a brief encounter with Christianity. She began looking for the twenty who participated in the private home venture. She found many of these and added more until she gathered a group of fifty of the poorest children with which to start the feeding center.

Then, she told the squatters to move so that construction of the building could begin. The squatters refused to cooperate. Sister Birdie tried to explain that it was for the betterment of the village. This property was also the normal pathway to the main road. Consequently, everyone in the surrounding area became upset when they realized that they would have to walk around the new construction.

However, the worst problem was the little old man who had lived near the coconut trees for twenty-five years. Appeasing him almost started a battle. Eventually, Sister Birdie helped all the people, including the little old man, relocate their homes to a nearby spot. A property line was established, and construction began.

The first job was to build a wall eight to ten feet high to keep the people out while the building was being constructed. Theft was a tremendous problem. Also, the wall would be used to keep out the thousands of children whom the center could not afford to feed.

Sister Birdie ordered the exact amounts of rock and cement needed. Anything extra would be stolen overnight. She set a time for delivery. Getting the supplies in on the narrow, mud roads presented a challenge. She waited hours for the first shipment, but it never arrived. Finally, she caught a bus, made a transfer, and eventually arrived at the contractor's office. She demanded, "Where are our supplies?"

The contractor looked perplexed. "But ma'am, our truck was turned back. We tried to deliver them earlier today, and an elderly gentleman said the project had been canceled."

Sister Birdie shouted, "He has no authority. I am the one

in charge. Please deliver the supplies tomorrow personally to me."

The shipment arrived, and the first stones were set in place. The old man appointed himself supervisor and complained that the stones were too close to his coconut trees. Sister Birdie learned to work around him with a minimum of confrontation.

The workmen erected a ten-foot stone wall and assembled a small thatched hut in one corner. From this shack, the first fifty children received a lunch consisting of a small bowl of rice and a glass of milk. The children whose homes adjoined the property line were included in this feeding program. Many of the mothers were given jobs cooking and serving the food, which allowed them to be fed too. The program soon grew to include 150 children. In time, Sister Birdie and her thatched hut feeding program were accepted and welcomed by the surrounding community.

Chapter Nine

The Miracle of the Film

Elaine and I spent our time going back and forth to Sri Lanka. Late one night after returning to California, I was suffering from jet lag. I turned on the TV and watched a show presented by Art Beales, the president of World Concern. His words caught my attention: "In the next hour, I will show the needs of children around the world and tell how you can help."

The film showed vocational training, feeding centers, and health programs in various parts of the world. I thought, *That's exactly what we are doing. I wonder if World Concern would help us?*

After the program, a number to call for pledge donations flashed on the screen. When I called, the operator referred me to the business office in Seattle. I copied down the telephone number and placed it on my desk.

A few days later, we planned our next overseas trip. I cleaned the desktop and discovered the forgotten World Concern number. My watch showed 4:55 PM, but I hoped someone would still be in the office. I dialed the number.

Instead of reaching a switchboard operator, a man with a British accent answered. "Hello, this is Barry Iison. Can I help you?"

I said, "I watched your hour-long TV special the other night. Do you offer help to outside missionaries?"

He did not answer directly. Instead, he asked me many questions which seemed remote at the time. We talked for a while, and I discovered that he had grown up in Bangladesh where his parents were missionaries. Currently, he was Foreign Director of Educational and Vocational Training for World Concern.

I explained our ministry to him. "Our feeding program includes approximately 270 children. Our centers are growing faster than we can raise sponsors. I hope your organization will be able to help us. Could I possibly find an answer before I return to Sri Lanka next week?"

Barry replied, "That would be impossible. We are a large organization. It takes time to process all the necessary forms and receive committee approval for new projects."

I persisted, "If your filming crew had come through Sri Lanka and seen our work, I'm sure we would have been on that TV special. Coverage like that would help our ministry unbelievably."

"Sometime soon we'll be filming in Somalia and Lebanon," he said.

Suddenly I felt desperate. "For God's sake, Barry, don't leave us alone in Sri Lanka. If you have the ability, please help us."

"I'll see what I can do."

I was in my office the day after Thanksgiving. Everyone except Elaine and me had gone home early. At 5:05 PM, I held my briefcase in my hand and was reaching for the doorknob when the phone rang.

I looked at Elaine and said, "I'd better answer it. It might be a crisis."

Elaine frowned. "What can you do? We're leaving for Sri Lanka in a few hours."

I felt compelled to answer the telephone. "I can take the information and refer it to another pastor." I picked up the receiver and said, "This is Deo Miller."

A voice responded, "Hello, this is Barry Iison from World Concern. We'll have a film crew in Africa soon. The director, Bob Screen, would like to see your project when he finishes over there. I'll telex his time of arrival."

"That's wonderful, Barry. How will I identify the man?"

Barry laughed. "Don't worry. You'll recognize him."

I left for Sri Lanka, still wondering what to expect from Bob Screen and his crew. A few days later, I received a telex: Bob Screen—Arrival 5:00 PM—December 2—Colombo.

Elaine and I, wanting to impress Bob and his crew, dressed in our best clothes. The decision concerning whether or not the film would be made lay in his power. Our driver arrived late as usual with some flimsy excuse, resulting in one of his famous maniacal drives from downtown Colombo to the airport twenty-two miles away. The highway was only one lane wide. Whenever another car approached, we veered onto the shoulder. The driver dodged ox carts filled with sunbaked roofing tile and pedestrians balancing trays of fruits and vegetables on their shoulders. Weaving back and forth over the narrow road, he determined to reach the airport before our important guests arrived.

When we approached the airport gate, the guards seemed in no hurry to let us through. For security precautions, a special pass costing five rupees was required to enter the terminal. As the guard was asking to see the telex, we were anxiously watching Bob's flight land on the single runway.

Finally the guard waved us through the gate. Our driver screeched up to the loading area and slammed on the brakes. Dust flew in all directions. Two more guards with fixed rifles took our passes and opened the airport terminal doors.

Just as we rushed to the railing, a six-foot-nine-inch man with light brown hair and a beaming smile entered the baggage claim area. We knew he was Bob Screen.

We shook hands and welcomed him to Sri Lanka. Our driver drove us to the Oberoi Hotel where we left Bob to get some rest after his long flight from the Seychelles Islands.

The next day, we took him on a tour of our feeding centers. At this point, our buildings were only a cluster of reed frames covered with palm fronds. I wondered what our guest thought about our small operation.

As if reading my mind and trying to put me at ease, he smiled and said, "I like what you are doing here."

Our last stop was the feeding center in Hell's Seventeen Acres. I explained to him why the ten-foot wall was necessary. "It's to prevent theft and to keep out the 5,800 children we aren't able to feed. Our hope is to feed more children and teach them vocational skills, particularly here in Hell's Seventeen Acres where the need is overwhelming."

Our driver dropped Bob at the Oberoi Hotel to freshen up for dinner before he returned us to our stifling hot flat. As soon as we dressed, we walked over to the hotel to wait for Bob in the air-conditioned lobby. When he joined us, I started talking about our feeding programs.

He interrupted me. "Listen, Deo. You don't have to sell me. I've seen what God has put together through you. Don't worry about getting my support. I see your need, and I'm sold on your program. Let's just relax and get to know each other, okay?"

What a delightful evening together it turned out to be! Bob stayed a few more days before leaving for Seattle. Elaine and I stayed another month, supervising the feeding programs and determining their needs.

A few weeks later, Art Beales wired us that he would be in Singapore and wanted us to join him for breakfast. We booked a flight for what became an interesting visit with the president of World Concern. He encouraged us and prayed with us. Then he smiled and said, "Somehow, God waived all the normal channels usually required to obtain aid from World Concern. You started at the top with Barry and me. It's a mystery how you reached Barry by dialing the switchboard number."

A few days after returning to Sri Lanka, Elaine and I became ill. We assumed it was the local flu since we had taken all the necessary shots for typhoid, cholera, and other tropical diseases. However, we both were bedridden until our return ticket date.

Still ill, we boarded the plane for the grueling thirty-eight-hour flight home. Neither of us was able to eat on the airplane. Arriving in California, we immediately went to the doctor's office and discovered that, in spite of the injections, we both had contracted typhoid fever. The doctor prescribed some medications and sent us home to bed.

Two days later, the phone rang. "This is Barry. Could you return to Sri Lanka in four days?"

Still exhausted from the typhoid, I asked, "What for?"

"The filming crew finished the job in Africa and could arrive at that time. Not only did Bob Screen say that there's a story worth telling, but Art Beales also recommended that World Concern fly you back over there for the filming."

We hadn't even had a chance to unpack our suitcases. Elaine and I were both physically drained in spite of the medication, but we knew this was a great opportunity. We flew back to Sri Lanka, logging 27,000 miles in ten days.

At that time, many considered Sri Lanka a major tourist island for the Europeans, comparing it to Hawaii with its sandy beaches, coconut palms, and hot weather. Secluded resorts were reasonably priced, their walls shutting out the poverty of Colombo. The government did not particularly want the world to see what was beyond those walls. For that reason, the news media was not welcome to see the unpleasant sections of Colombo.

When Bob asked if there would be any problem bringing the filming equipment into Sri Lanka, we asked Colton. He said there might be trouble, but we needed to trust God to work things out for us, because the film would greatly help our cause. I suggested to Bob that the equipment be disguised to prevent any problems with the customs officials, but I did not want him to know the gravity of the situation for fear he would not come.

Soon, we received a telex: Bob Screen—Arriving 11:00 PM—Please make arrangements to pick up seven men and equipment.

We arranged through Colton to rent a small bus. This time, we made sure the driver arrived early. We parked the bus directly in front of the baggage claim area, filling the entire curbside parking area of the small airport.

"Wait for us. Don't move that bus!" I instructed the driver as I climbed out.

Barefoot boys wearing cut-off pants greeted us, anxious to earn a few rupees carrying luggage. A few older boys wore thongs. They followed us through the double doors, the flip-flop of their thongs resounding on the terrazzo tile floor.

I saw Bob Screen talking to the customs officials on the other side of the glass partition. Normally, the Sri Lankan customs officials were soft spoken and cordial. We had never experienced any delay arriving or departing on any of our trips.

I glanced over at the rack where the film crew's luggage waited to be claimed. I counted thirty-five pieces, mostly huge footlockers. Pasted on the side of each one in big, bold letters was, "Video Equipment: Screen Communications."

I looked at Elaine and moaned, "Oh no! I asked them to camouflage it. We'll never clear all that equipment through customs. What are we going to do? The officials will confiscate it all!"

"Let's pray," my wife answered.

We held hands, and I prayed. "Dear Lord, please allow this filming crew and their thirty-five pieces of luggage to enter Sri Lanka. We trust you to open the doors for them."

I glanced nervously around the busy waiting room, crammed with about two hundred people. There were Europeans arriving for the Christmas holidays, Sri Lankans waiting for their loved ones, and businessmen leaving for distant cities. All chattered in their native languages.

I could see Bob and Art still talking to the customs officials through the glass partition. It was time for action. I boldly walked up to one of the rifle-bearing guards who stood in the doorway between the waiting room and the customs area.

"I have to get my friends there. The bus is waiting out front." Without giving him an opportunity to answer, I walked by him and clapped my hands in the air. Turning to the boys in cut-offs who were still behind me, I ordered, "Come on boys, let's get that luggage loaded. Come, come."

The boys, anticipating a large tip, raced over and began placing the mammoth footlockers on carts.

I walked up to the World Concern group. Smiling, I shook their hands and said, "Hello, Bob. Hello, Art. How are you?" Then, turning to the filming crew, I continued, "Come on, men. Don't ask questions. Follow me."

Bob and Art exchanged glances. They knew something was not quite right, but they obeyed my loud, authoritative voice and followed me out of the customs area.

The official tried to protest. "But wait, what. . . ."

I interrupted him, "Officer, I have the bus waiting for my friends. See, right there." Clapping my hands again and motioning to the boys, I shouted, "Come on, boys. Bring that luggage through the doors and load it on the bus."

The twenty-five-yard distance from where I stood, through the double doors, and past the armed guards was the longest walk of my life. I wondered if the customs official would tell the two guards to halt us. Instead, he followed me asking, "What is all this equipment? What is going on here?"

I said, "We're just doing a little work." Then motioning to the boys, "Quickly, quickly. Get that equipment loaded on the bus." I motioned to the filming crew to enter the bus.

Another customs official appeared. Elaine took over. "What's the weather been like? I hope I brought the right clothes. Where is a good place for us to dine?" She babbled on and on.

Amid all the confusion, both officials tried to answer my beautiful wife's barrage of questions while trying to find out what was happening.

When the equipment was loaded on the bus, I reached in my pocket and located a handful of ballpoint pens which were new to Sri Lanka. I handed several to the customs officials. Then I gave extra rupees and a ballpoint pen to each of the boys who had somehow wedged all thirty-five pieces of luggage into the small bus.

Art and Bob climbed aboard. Elaine and I followed. I looked out the window at the customs men saying in my most cordial voice, "Thank you for all your cooperation, men. My friends are looking forward to their visit in your beautiful country."

The bus pulled away, leaving two perplexed customs officials on the curb. Cold perspiration trickled down my neck and into my shirt collar. I felt tired and had not slept for four nights. The typhoid fever raged within me. Slumping into my seat, I looked at Art Beales seated across the aisle.

He said, "I don't know what's going on here, but I think I've just seen a miracle."

I returned his knowing look. Words were unnecessary.

After safely depositing our guests at the Oberoi Hotel, we went home to our flat and collapsed on the bed.

The next morning, we entered the lobby of the hotel to breakfast with our guests. As I walked past the check-in counter, the clerk stopped me and asked, "Oh sir, sir. Are you part of the filming crew?"

I did not know what to answer, so I said, "Well, ahhhhhhh."

He continued, "Are you part of that group that arrived last night?"

"Yes, I am," I admitted.

He persisted, "Are you part of the telecommunications group that's arriving? You are here three days early, aren't you? I suppose you have come to help us understand our new TV and radio system."

"No, I'm with a different group," I answered. Suddenly I realized how this miracle had taken place. The airport customs officials thought we were part of the expected radio and TV group. That is why we slid through customs without having the equipment confiscated or without posting bond for it.

Three days later, the telecommunications people arrived with ten times more equipment than the World Concern filming crew. I looked at Elaine and said, "Wow! That's who they thought we were."

In the meantime, the World Concern crew filmed our feeding center at Hell's Seventeen Acres. The local people willingly cooperated. We paid a few rupees to everyone who appeared in the film. Everything ran smoothly.

Trenches for the foundation of the feeding center had been dug, but additional funds were necessary to build the structure. One hundred and fifty children continued to be fed under the grass shack.

Art Beales said, "You know, Deo, we made the film; but we need to do something more."

We had talked previously with him about developing skills in the children, but we did not have enough funds to begin. Coming from a construction background, I appreciated the need for the children to learn lifelong trades. Elaine felt her teaching background would be helpful in setting up programs too.

Art wrote a check. Handing it to me, he said, "This should cover the purchase of ten sewing machines. When you return home, come to my office in Seattle. I'll see that you receive a grant to start a vocational training program here in Hell's Seventeen Acres."

"Thank you, Art. I really appreciate your generosity and your interest in our program." I knew that World Concern was going to use the film for its own TV broadcast so I asked, "Would it also be possible for me to get a copy of the film to use when I speak in churches?"

Shortly thereafter, we returned to the U.S. Bob Screen called a month later and said, "Deo, the film is almost completed. The air date will be September 24. The total cost was $50,000, which includes airfares, hotel bills, and salaries as well as film production. Art Beales wants you and Elaine to come to the headquarters in Seattle as soon as possible."

I thanked him and hung up. I had not realized the cost involved. How could I pay for a $50,000 film? That was larger than our yearly budget.

I prayed about this new problem on the flight to Seattle. When we arrived, the staff at World Concern greeted us warmly. We met with Art and filled out the forms for the grant he promised.

The next day, we lunched with Bob. I sheepishly asked, "How's the film coming along?"

He answered, "It's ready to be aired on TV in six thousand cities. By the way, you were questioning the cost." He looked at me.

A cold sweat crept over my back. I nodded my head thinking, *Here comes the bill.*

Bob continued, "We talked it over and have decided to give you the film. We will produce it on sixteen-millimeter film in full color, professionally edited to twelve minutes, so you can use it in your speaking engagements."

He watched my sigh of relief. "That's how much we think of your ministry, Deo. The people who worked with you in Sri Lanka want to donate their time. Some are absorbing their costs. World Concern has offered to pay the balance of the bill."

We thanked him and telexed Colton to share the good news of receiving the free film and the promise of a grant. The money raised from the airing of our show would fund the grant.

Going home on the plane that evening, I thought about what had just happened. Back in Sri Lanka several months before, on the bus as we were leaving Colombo airport, Art Beales had said, "I think I've just seen a miracle." I think he was right.

But if he had seen one, then Elaine and I had seen at least three! The first one was the day God allowed my phone call to get through, making it possible for me to meet directly with the president of World Concern instead of going through the slow, normal channels.

Second, the Lord had transported the film crew in and out of Sri Lanka with no hassle from customs. That had to be a miracle in itself.

But little had we dreamed of how much it would really cost World Concern to produce that film. The fact that they had given us a copy of it at no cost was not only the third miracle, but also a very precious and encouraging gift to us and our work.

Chapter Ten

The Ambassador

Elaine and I continued our journeys back and forth to Sri Lanka, raising funds on one shore and supervising the expansion of work on the other.

The project called Hell's Seventeen Acres continued to go well under the supervision of Sister Birdie. By then the work had expanded to a multifaceted center.

Late one afternoon, a thin, hollow-cheeked woman walked into Sister Birdie's office, tightly gripping her youngest child's hand. Four other children shuffled in behind her. Their young mother seated herself in a wooden chair across from Sister Birdie.

The woman's matted hair hung in clumps around her shoulders. Nervously, she twisted a piece of paper in her hand as she began to speak. "My husband's disappeared. He's an alcoholic. He's left before, but usually he comes home after a few days. Now he's been gone three months. I don't think he will return. My children are starving, but I can't work. Who will take care of my young ones?" The desperation in her eyes pleaded with the center director.

Sister Birdie looked sadly at the helpless woman, thinking of all the families who suffered because of fathers who were addicted to the local coconut liquor. The thinning, ginger-colored hair and bloated stomachs of the three youngest children showed the telltale signs of malnutrition. Their bodies retained fluid, giving them a deceptively healthy appearance, but their faces portrayed the haunting look of hunger.

The director sighed. How many more children could she add to her overcrowded program? Glancing at the three youngest ones, she knew she had to accept them. The older two would survive by begging, stealing, or working part-time. Their malnutrition did not seem as pronounced as that of the younger children. Sister Birdie replied, "I can accept your three youngest children into our program."

Tears filled the mother's eyes, "Oh, thank you. Thank you," she softly answered. Her resigned expression changed to one of expectation and joy.

Sister Birdie's goal was to include children in the center's program before the ravages of malnutrition set in deeply. Long-term malnutrition affected children mentally, making them lethargic. Malnourished children around the world are often incorrectly diagnosed as being mentally retarded. Sister Birdie prayed that it was not too late for these little ones.

The center fed and clothed the youngest member of this family, Dakatta. He was two years old.

His nine-year-old sister, Sisira, entered the vocational sewing program. First she practiced stitching buttons on small scraps of cloth donated by garment shops. Having never seen a needle and thread before, Sisira needed to develop the eye-hand coordination of hand sewing. Over and over, she practiced sewing the squares together until they would not come apart. When Sisira connected enough multicolored pieces together to measure two to three yards, she hemmed it, creating her first skirt. The entire process took almost six months.

By the time Sisira completed her skirt of many colors, her bloated stomach was gone. Her hair had begun to thicken and return to its natural, black color. Her eyes sparkled, and smiles brought dimples to the corners of her mouth as signs of malnutrition vanished.

Next, Sisira moved into the sewing room where the Singer foot treadle machines were located. She learned to keep her fingers out of the way of the moving needle. A pile of scraps became another patchwork garment. Once she accomplished this task, she was given one and one-half yards of purchased fabric. She learned to measure herself for a pattern and cut out a frock. When she finished her own dress, she sewed clothing for some younger girls in the center.

Sisira's brother, Ransinghe, with his wide cheekbones, curly hair, and broad nose was tall and sinewy, looking older than his eleven years. His introduction to the center was the beginner's woodworking class. After the prayer and study time each morning, the boys were given their assignments for the day. The more experienced boys often were assigned to work with the younger ones. The instructor helped Ransinghe on his first day by giving him a pattern and teaching him to trace it on a block of wood.

Using a chisel and a mallet, Ransinghe cut around his design. His work was crude at first, but he kept trying. Soon, he created a plaque with his name chiseled on it. After learning to use a hammer and a saw, he crafted a spoon.

Ransinghe made many mistakes in the beginning because his left-hand to right-hand coordination was so bad. Also his hands and eyes needed practice working together. Lots of scrap wood resulted, but he learned. After several months, the eleven-year-old had built his own tool box.

When he became competent with hand tools, he progressed into the power tool room, where he observed a lathe for several days. The older, experienced boys explained what to do and not to do. Ransinghe's fingers were at stake. When he thoroughly understood the machinery, he was allowed to use the lathe to build furniture.

Within a year, a boy Ransinghe's age could handcraft decent furniture to be sold by the church. After several years, the handmade furniture was nice enough to grace any living room. By then, the young man had enough skills to leave the center and to earn his own living, perhaps starting his own small furniture-making business. In many cases, his paycheck would bring enough rice and vegetables to feed and clothe his entire family and more.

The older girls graduated into a classroom with commercial sewing machines. The Hell's Seventeen Acres Center owned only a few of these more costly machines. A number of Japanese garment factories located in Sri Lanka offered good jobs to girls who knew how to sew commercially.

Many villages didn't have even one sewing machine in the entire community. Some girls living in more remote areas preferred to start their own sewing businesses in their huts. In these instances, each seamstress was allowed to take a sewing machine with her when she left the center. This created a constant need to purchase new machines. If a girl stayed in the program two years, the sewing machine was donated to her with the stipulation that she would never sell or trade it. By sewing and mending garments, a sixteen-year-old girl can support her mother and a number of sisters and brothers. If the family moves, the girl takes the sewing machine with her and can earn a living anywhere. Once she marries, she continues her work as seamstress, often supporting her entire family.

Because of the shortage of sewing machines, most centers offer other forms of sewing. After learning the hand sewing, some of the girls transfer to a crocheting room. The instructor teaches each girl to shape a set of six coasters for her first project. Usually, no two coasters are alike on the first attempt. Yet, after six months, a girl can fashion beautifully matching sets.

Then she graduates to a different grade of yarn and, using the same pattern, she crochets a handmade tablecloth. These beautiful pieces of artwork usually take about nine months to complete.

Some of the older girls attend lacemaking classes. The machine for making the lace looks something like a hand-operated knitting machine. Sixty oblong bobbins of various thicknesses of nylon thread hang in a row from the top. The girl sits on a stool and weaves the bobbins in and out, creating a pattern of one-inch-wide handmade lace. Lace is expensive in Sri Lanka. A hand machine for lace-making can be inexpensively set up for each girl to take home and start her own lacemaking business.

Life and activity in the feeding centers revolve around the church that sponsors the center. Each church holds a bazaar so that the coasters, placemats, tablecloths, doilies, pillowcases, and napkin-ring-holders can be sold to raise money for the feeding programs. The funds are also used to buy new sewing supplies. Plaques, spoons, chairs, tables, sewing boxes, and clothes racks crafted in the woodworking shop are sold to raise money for more wood.

The teachers in the sewing and woodworking classes, all Christians, are experts in their fields; and they also provide spiritual support for the children. Each class begins with prayer and a short Bible lesson. The leaders become personally involved in the children's lives, bringing the message of Jesus Christ to each individual.

Education is free in Sri Lanka, but if a child drops out of school due to sickness or malnutrition, no provision is made for reentry. Illiterate parents rarely stress the importance of attending school regularly, so truancy becomes another obstacle to the education of children.

Most of the children who end up in the feeding centers have dropped out of school, the main reason why vocational training is so important in helping them establish their own occupations. The feeding centers bring the good news to these children and make them productive people in their own communities. Hungry children can't be taught; but once the pain of hunger vanishes and they realize that someone cares, they become teachable.

Bible story pictures provide an excellent tool of evangelism in all the centers. With the help of leaders, the children draw scenes and people from the Bible. Often the leaders write Bible verses on the bottom of the paper. Every illustration that goes home will probably be looked at by seven adults. Many of the Scripture drawings will hang on the walls of the huts, visually spreading the gospel.

Because each feeding center is part of a local Christian church instead of an outside organization, the center exerts a tremendous impact on the community. The program runs Monday through Friday and is not meant to be a welfare program. The nighttime and weekend responsibilities for the children fall on the parents. The children always live and sleep in their own homes.

The centers focus on feeding, vocational training, and medical assistance. However, the greatest impact is that the children come to know the love of Jesus through their Christian leaders who care for each of them individually. Most of the children and their parents become Christians as a result.

Many young people who graduate from the vocational training program at age fifteen continue to attend church. If they move to another community, they often return from time to time to visit their center leaders and pastors.

Elaine and I originally hoped that the feeding centers would ultimately pay for themselves. Yet, for every ten who graduate from a center, fifty are waiting to take their places in the vocational training programs.

Once, when Elaine and I planned to return to the U.S. for an extended visit, we stopped by each feeding center to say good-bye to the children on our way to the airport. Our last stop was Hell's Seventeen Acres. We arrived in the van, and Sister Birdie greeted us with an enormous hug. We said hello to the children who were waiting in line for lunch. They waved and smiled. When we entered each classroom, I said a few words of encouragement. "Keep up the good work. That's beautiful. Your work is professional."

I felt it was important for these young people to know that others were giving to help support what we were doing, and that it was more than Elaine's and my money.

Entering the power tool area where the most advanced

boys worked, I said, "We come to you as ambassadors. We represent many Americans who make your program work. We are not overseers. Your leaders and teachers are all Sri Lankans. Our job is to love you, to care for you, and to see that you are taught a skill."

A boy about the age of thirteen raised his hand. Sister Birdie looked startled. Normally, the children were extremely shy and never spoke. He stood up and began to talk. "Remember when I used to spend all my time on the dirt road near here, running with a street gang?"

To be honest, I could not recall. There were so many boys, but I nodded my head so he could continue.

"I was always in trouble with people in the village," he continued. "One day, you came down the road and invited me to join your program and learn woodworking. I want you to know that I represent these boys. You could say that I'm the ambassador for this classroom, because I speak for everyone here.

"Sir, you brought something more important than the workworking shop or the sewing center upstairs, or even the food center. I came here with no clothing. Sister Birdie gave me clothes. I didn't eat regularly. Now I eat every day. I was sick, and the doctor made me well. But more important than all these things is the teacher who came to instruct us about a man called Jesus."

"How does your teacher help you?" I asked.

"My professor prays with me each morning. He prays with every boy in this class. He explained to me who Jesus Christ is. He told us that you came because Jesus Christ loves you, you love Him, and you love us.

"Now, I have Jesus Christ living in me! I know Him personally, just as you know Him. That, sir, is the most important thing you have done. Your message has changed our lives. We want to thank you from the bottom of our hearts. You came to me and my brothers and showed that you care. Thank you, sir, for being our ambassador."

Chapter Eleven

Two Rupees for Surakata

The model stepped onto the stage and whirled around to the beat of exotic, Oriental music. Elaine read: "Sonja is wearing a gorgeous, hand-crocheted marvel that you'll love to own. Since each dress is handmade, no two are alike. These dresses are available in white, beige, or black and in small, medium, and large. A teenager in one of our centers spent eight months crocheting this beautiful garment. The hand washable ensemble will be on sale immediately following the fashion show. Remember—when you purchase a dress, you feed a child in Sri Lanka."

I sat in the audience of more than one thousand women watching my beautiful wife present a fashion show fundraiser for our ministry. Before we married, Elaine modeled clothes. She had an excellent eye for color and design. I thought of how perfectly her talents fitted into our ministry.

I continued to daydream, recalling our first dinner in Sri Lanka nine years before where we saw a fashion show. The next day, Elaine purchased a batik skirt and a hand-crocheted dress. While wearing these elegant garments in the U.S., she often received compliments. Many friends said, "Next time you go to Sri Lanka, bring me one." Soon, she was purchasing dresses for others. Before long, she received more requests than she could handle.

One night Elaine suggested, "Deo, perhaps I should consider doing fashion shows and selling the clothes to raise money for the children. I could buy the garments wholesale, add the price of feeding a child for a month, and sell them inexpensively."

I encouraged her to pursue the idea. The next time Colton and Suzanne visited, they brought a suitcase full of dresses. Elaine presented the first fashion show locally in a friend's church. The event raised seven hundred dollars, an overwhelming response.

Soon Elaine was presenting two or three fashion shows a month. Her garments included designs from all over the world—Hong Kong, Singapore, Jakarta, India, Sri Lanka, and southern California. Colorful batiks, embroidered skirts, and crocheted dresses were some of the unusual choices available.

These fashion shows, along with my speaking engagements, provided most of the funds for Hope Child Care International Ministries. The World Concern film was shown every time we spoke. Often after people see the movie, they realize the plight of our children, and many are moved to become sponsors. Others buy a new dress or give a one-time donation.

Today we offer a variety of programs. The largest feeding center is located in Hell's Seventeen Acres, now serving hundreds of children. In place of the original grass shack, a two-story center now stands. The sewing rooms are upstairs; the woodworking shop and kitchen are downstairs.

Some centers allow children to participate in an afterschool program where they eat lunch, benefit from the religious training, and learn some of the lesser skills. In a few centers the younger children are taught how to plant seeds in pots and care for them with water and fertilizer. The grown flower and vegetable plants are sold at church bazaars.

In the outer villages the children speak less English. An instructor assigned to each center teaches the children to read and write English. One village needed secretaries, so the center purchased typewriters. Girls at thirteen or fourteen learn typing skills. Education is the main concern of this center. Secretarial jobs are readily offered to these girls when they graduate.

The Sumith Center, located near a river, emphasizes the craft of mat-making. Children first learn to weave reeds into placemats. Eventually they progress to constructing large rug mats. These beautifully designed floor mats are sold to a rug dealer.

Surakata, a friendly ten-year-old boy, attends the Sumith Center. Whenever Elaine and I visit, Surakata waves and greets us with a wide grin. He often tells us about his family and his current project at the center. Last year he mastered weaving placemats and began his first ten-by-ten-foot floor mat.

Shortly after we finished our fund-raising tour of the United States in 1987, we returned to Sri Lanka. On our first tour of the feeding centers, we stopped by the Sumith Center. A delicious aroma filled the air as Elaine and I stepped from the van.

Lunch, bought fresh every day by staff members, simmered in large kettles over propane burners. A meal for several hundred children required four to five hours of preparation time. Each vegetable simmered in a separate pot with onions, chili peppers, and curry added for taste. I smelled potatoes, leeks, carrots, and rice—the mainstay of their diet.

Some of the younger children sat on the long benches, eating the meal with their fingers. Lunch was served at about two-thirty or three in the afternoon in the Sri Lankan custom. The center in Hell's Seventeen Acres provides tables as well as benches, but most centers only have benches. Children may take seconds or thirds as long as they do not waste food.

A huge bowl of rice sat in the center of each plate. The curried fish, hard-boiled egg, and curried vegetables formed a circle around the rice. When finished, the children washed their own bowls and plates under the water tap and stacked them in a pile. After lunch, everyone gathered for religious training before going home for the day.

We waved to the small children. They stopped eating long enough to smile and wave back. Then we walked into the mat-making room. I expected to be greeted by Surakata with a progress report on his rug mat. However, he was not there. I asked the director, "Do you know where Surakata is?"

She shrugged her shoulders and replied, "He might be sick, or maybe he's running errands for his mother."

Although we emphasize regular attendance, sometimes the parents do not understand the importance of a daily commitment to the program. If they need work done at home or help with the younger children, they ask the boy or girl to stay home for a day.

About a week later, we returned to the Sumith Center. Surakata was still missing.

The center leader said, "Deo, we're worried now about Surakata. He attended regularly. It's not like him to be absent over a week. If I give you directions to his home, will you stop by this afternoon?"

I nodded. Elaine and I climbed in the van and I instructed the driver who drove us through the lush jungle growing along the riverside. The narrow road wound back and forth, following the meandering river to the village where Surakata lived.

The driver parked. I walked up the crooked trail leading to the village. A woman who was washing her clothes in the river directed me to the hut where Surakata lived. Surakata's mother sat outside the shanty. She rocked back and forth, tightly clutching her knees in her arms. A low moan escaped from her lips. Tears streamed down her cheeks.

I walked up to her and placed my hand on her shoulder. "Hello. I'm Deo Miller from the Sumith Center. We've missed Surakata. Where is he?"

"He's terribly sick" was the mother's tired response. "I don't know what's wrong with him."

"Where is he?" I repeated.

"He's lying inside on the floor," she answered, motioning to the entrance of her home.

I entered the hot, musty hut, bending down as I walked through the low doorway. When my eyes became adjusted to the dark interior, I saw Surakata curled up on a mat in the corner. His body was contorted into an unnatural position. I tried to speak to him, but he was unaware of my presence. His forehead burned with fever.

I picked up the semiconscious boy, mat and all, and carried him out of the stifling hut. I laid him gently on the ground near his mother. He remained in the strange, fetal position, unable to move or communicate.

"How long has he been like this?" I asked.

"Almost a week. I can't break the fever." The mother's penetrating eyes searched mine for reassurance. She asked, "Will Surakata die?"

I could not meet her gaze. Instead, I stared in horror at the distorted figure before me. "I'll take him to the hospital. I have a car here. Do you have a blanket that I can wrap him in?"

The woman entered her house and returned with a tattered piece of fabric. I wrapped the frail body and gently lifted Surakata into my arms. Carefully I hiked down the winding path to the van.

When the driver saw the seriousness of the situation, he gunned the engine, winding us through the traffic in our makeshift ambulance. A nurse greeted us at the emergency entrance of the large, white goverment hospital. Upon seeing the boy, she shook her head. "No hope, no hope."

Ignoring her diagnosis, I signed the necessary forms to admit the gravely ill boy for treatment. Then, Elaine and I returned to our flat, leaving Surakata in the hands of God and the hospital staff.

Elaine and I often prayed for this friendly little boy. Soon I found time to visit Surakata again. Entering the government hospital, I discovered a maze of corridors with no central information center and no signs. However, I knew there must be a children's ward. I wound my way through building after building, wing after wing. At first, I did not see any nurses or children. An overflow of beds spilled into the hallways. Apparently every bed was filled, because many patients reclined on mats on the floor.

Finally, I located a nurse in a large ward on the third floor. She motioned down another corridor and pointed upstairs. When I reached the end of the hallway, I heard the chatter and laughter of children filtering down the staircase. I climbed the stairs to the fourth floor. I finally had found the children's area.

The place reeked of Lysol. There were no doors on the rooms. Each ward contained twenty-five to thirty beds. The iron-rail frames, painted white long ago, were cracked and peeling. Thin, two-inch mattresses rested on the metal frames.

Few children were in bed. Most ran up and down the halls, acting as if they were out for recess. I saw no nurses.

I walked into the next ward and finally found a nurse who knew Surakata. She said, "He had an attack of rheumatic fever. He is weak, so we suspect there is a hole in his heart. He needs total bed rest and no activity for many months."

She showed me Surakata's bed. It was empty. We found him in the hall chasing another boy. I gave the nurse a disapproving glance. Then I noticed her lined face and wondered what working in this bedlam would be like.

The nurse shrugged her stooped shoulders and said flatly, "I have fifty children to take care of by myself. I do the best I can."

I took Surakata by the hand and led him back to his bed. I gently said, "Surakata, I'm glad you are feeling better, but you look tired."

He nodded in agreement.

I continued, "The only way you will get well is to take care of yourself. You have to rest in bed all the time until you are strong. When you feel better, you can return to the Sumith Center. But you must do your part."

I sat on the edge of the bed and hugged this special boy. The doctor's report stated that Surakata's eyes had crossed due to the muscle spasms and fever. I knew this condition would probably never be corrected, but at least he was alive. "I brought you some sweets and a coloring book and crayons. You can color in bed and learn to reuse your eyes again."

"Uncle Deo, I no see good," was the meek reply.

"You do what I tell you, and you'll be home soon."

He grinned. "OK, Uncle Deo. I rest."

Six weeks later, the hospital released the young boy. I visited his home and emphasized the doctor's advice to his mother. "Surakata can't fetch water from the river or carry firewood. Making him do heavy labor of any kind will kill him. His older sister can bring food home from the center for him each day."

His mother nodded and said, "I promise to let him rest. My husband left us last year. It is difficult to get the chores done, but the other children can help. I want my son to live."

I stared at her, trying to phrase my next words. I knew Surakata had participated in the center's program for almost six months. "When Surakata first became sick, why didn't you tell someone at the center? Why didn't you do something?"

She looked guilty and hung her head. "He was sick before, but he always got well. I gave him the herbs from the priest, but this time they didn't help. He burned up with fever. He got sicker."

"We told you to come to the center whenever you have a problem. Why didn't you come?"

The mother shook her head. Sickness was a way of life in her village. "I didn't want to bother them. I thought the herbs would make him well."

I shivered. The folk religion of the Sinhalese people blends with their Buddhist faith. They worship an assortment of local gods, the most dramatic of which involves the exorcism of demons and spirits believed to be the cause of disease. Magical practices enhanced by elaborate dancing and drum rituals are used by local priests. Home remedies include herbal drinks and the application of oils and plasters.

In contrast, we arranged for doctors and nurses to pay regular visits to our feeding centers, usually once a week. Some of the larger centers require more frequent visits for ongoing problems. Nurses instruct the students in personal hygiene and dispense high protein vitamins. The doctors treat cuts, rat bites, and burns from open fires. They check for lice and worms, dispense needed medicine, and give inoculations. Yet, all the doctors in Sri Lanka fight a constant battle against the fears and religious beliefs of the people.

Exasperation welled up in me as I watched the reaction of Surakata's mother. "Why didn't you take him to the hospital? Why didn't you catch a bus to the government hospital? Treatment is free only a few miles away!"

She hung her head again and mumbled something. I knew many of these people were superstitious and regarded the hospital as a place to go to die. Many people never take advantage of the free medical services available.

"I can't hear you," I persisted. "Why didn't you take your ill son to the hospital?"

Her sad eyes met my gaze as she softly replied, "I would have taken him, but I didn't have two rupees."

Suddenly I understood. The bus fare to the hospital was one rupee each way. Surakata almost died because his mother did not have eight cents for bus fare.

Several months later Surakata returned to the Sumith Center. He was not allowed to play, but he could study and learn in spite of his crossed eyes. Today he is still in the center. Every time he sees Elaine and me, he smiles and waves. He has cheerfullly accepted his limited physical capabilities.

Shortly after this incident we returned to the U.S. for another fund-raising tour. One day I stood on a street corner watching two boys buy ice cream cones. They each received a double-dipper cone and a dime in change. One of the dimes slipped out of the boy's hand and rolled under a parked car. He looked at his friend, shrugged his shoulders, and walked away. Retrieving the dime was not worth his effort.

I thought of how Surakata almost died for the lack of eight cents. I wondered how many other children would die in poverty from a lack of bus fare to the hospital.

PFAFF

Chapter Twelve

Through the Eyes of Dinesha

Hundreds of children swarmed around the gates of the Hell's Seventeen Acres Center each time we visited there. Their palms turned upward; they stared at us. When Elaine and I stepped from the van, a feeling of inadequacy swept over me. I prayed, "Dear Lord, please provide a way for us to include these children in our feeding program"

But there was nothing I could do back then. Elaine and I stopped by the center to say good-bye to the children on our way to the airport. When we returned to America, we would share our concern for these little ones, starving outside the walls of our largest feeding center. Perhaps when we saw them again, we would no longer have to shut the steel gates in their faces.

The aroma of curry and peppers filled the air. The gate slammed behind us. The younger children sat at tables, eating their lunch of rice, fish, leeks, and hardboiled eggs. They smiled and waved. One shouted, "Hello, Aunt Elaine. Hello, Uncle Deo." I stopped to shake hands with some. As I walked by, I patted others on the head.

Sister Birdie rushed out and wrapped her massive arms around each of us in a bear hug. "Come and see the progress on our new vocational training center." She pointed in the direction of the construction.

The foundation was laid, but further progress would take more funds than were readily available. Meanwhile, seven hundred children were cramped into the original building meant to serve two to three hundred. Our mission in the U.S. on this trip home would be to raise money for the new 10,000-square-foot vocational training center.

Elaine stayed with Sister Birdie while I entered the woodworking shop. There, two boys deftly carved the legs on a table. A younger boy shyly handed me a crude wooden plaque. I asked, "Did you make this?"

He lowered his head and replied, "A gift for you, Uncle Deo."

I hugged the thin youngster and rumpled his hair. "Why, thank you. How thoughtful." Then glancing at the older boys, I said, "That table looks professionally done. Keep up the good work."

The woodworking instructor walked up to me and shook hands. I remarked, "That table is beautiful. Anyone would be proud to display it in his home. These boys have learned a great deal under your able instruction. I thank God for you and your talents."

Gratitude shone in the instructor's eyes as he said, "They are good workers. Rarely do they miss a day of training. Eventually, all my boys will be able to support their own families."

I looked around the room at the lathe, power saw, and other tools, remembering the day when this feeding center began with one determined lady and a grass feeding shack.

Elaine met me outside, and together we climbed the stairs to the sewing center to tell the girls good-bye. Elaine walked into the room that housed the sewing machines. I entered the crocheting room and watched busy hands at work.

One little girl looked up and smiled. I sat in an empty chair next to her. I could tell she was Hindu by the family mark on her forehead. Seated on my other side was a Muslim girl with whom I had chatted on my last visit. I looked around the room, noticing the many different nationalities and religions represented in the center.

The Sinhalese make up 70 percent of the population of Sri Lanka, and most are Buddhists. The Hindu Tamils make up 20 percent. The other 10 percent are divided evenly between Islam and Christianity.

A child's background has never been a factor in determining entry into a center. Their family need and our ability to include them are the only considerations. Once in the program, children form cross-cultural friendships.

Looking once again at the Hindu girl, I told her how I admired the tablecloth she was finishing. After two years in the program, her work looked professional. The girl who smiled at me was apparently attempting her first tablecloth. It was half completed. I could see that her hand stitching became progressively better as the tablecloth grew.

I examined the designs on the tablecloths, showing interest in each girl's hard work. After a few minutes, the little Hindu girl touched my arm and pointed to another girl sitting by herself in the corner. She whispered, "She's quite keen on learning to sew. Did you know that she is crippled?"

I looked over and recognized the girl. "Oh, yes. That's Dinesha. She's been in our program about a year."

Dinesha sensed that we were talking about her. She bowed her head and covered her deformed leg with the tablecloth she was making. Her little toes stuck out the bottom. Tears filled her large, brown eyes and trickled down her cheeks.

I said good-bye to the two girls. Walking over to Dinesha, I sat down next to her. She continued to stare at the floor. I felt her trembling body as I put my arm around her and hugged her. I said, "They weren't making fun of you. They're your friends. They didn't want me to leave without telling you good-bye."

Dinesha smiled, blinking back tears.

"You are very special to this class and to me. There is not

another little girl or boy who has a leg like yours. To me, you're one of the most beautiful little girls in the class."

"Do you really think so?" she shyly asked, her head still bowed.

"Yes, I do," I said emphatically. "Do you remember what I said when you first came to the center?"

"Yes. You told me that Jesus loves me."

"Why do you believe that Jesus loves you?"

"You told me so," she softly replied. "And my teacher tells me that each of us is special to Jesus."

While I was talking to Dinesha, Elaine came into the room and visited a group of girls in the corner. About twenty-five girls chatted in small groups around the crocheting classroom.

I continued, "No matter what takes place in life, and even though you have a leg that is not like anyone else's, God accepts you. And I accept you the way you are, too. Now that you've stopped crying, turn around in your seat and look at me."

I took Dinesha's hands in mine and swung her around, so I could look into her eyes. The minute that my eyes caught hers, something began to happen within me. Suddenly, she seemed to lose all facial features. A shiver went down my spine. It was as if the eyes no longer belonged to Dinesha.

All at once, I felt the presence of Jesus.

The eyes pierced through me. I could not look away. "Lord, what do you want of me?"

His glory seemed to overshadow everything around me. I was not aware of the other children in the room, or my wife, or the pressures of leaving for America. My total concentration focused on the eyes.

A voice within seemed to ask me, "Do you love this little girl?"

I replied, "Lord, you know I love her."

"Do you care for her?"

"Yes, I care. If I didn't, I wouldn't have bought her

crutches." I found myself justifying my concern for Dinesha.

"Do you accept her the way she is even though her leg is deformed?"

I said, "In my heart, I accept her the way she is. I don't see her as disabled."

Then it seemed the Lord said to me, "I accept you just the way you are, too."

I still could not remove my gaze from the penetrating eyes. The voice continued, "Do you know that you are crippled like this little girl? But you've covered it. You wear attractive clothing and nice shoes. You've placed a smile on your face. Physically, you don't appear deformed, but you're crippled more than this little girl."

"Lord, how can I be?"

"Because you are disabled in your heart," the answer seemed to say.

"In my heart?" I asked, pondering the words. Suddenly a vision of hundreds of little boxes appeared, memories I had stored away years before.

I thought of all the emotional hurts I had buried in my heart, the wrongdoings, the inadequacies, and the guilt hidden away long ago. Some of them hurt so badly, I didn't want to go through all the memories or face the past. In that moment, looking in the eyes of my little crippled friend, I realized all my deformities were just as visible to God as hers were to me.

Then the pictures of more past events, hurtful incidents, flashed through my mind in a matter of seconds. Memories of when I failed others and they failed me rose to accuse and haunt me. I saw a boss who mistreated me and my own anger over a silly occurrence. I recalled dark moments that I would have lived differently if the same situation developed today.

I also sensed as never before the compassion of Jesus. It seemed that in that moment He held a key in His outstretched hand that would open all the closed boxes, all the hurtful memories of the past.

Sitting there, still gazing into Dinesha's eyes, I, who had been trying to minister physically in Jesus' name, was being ministered to spiritually by the Lord himself. It was as if I heard Him say, "I've taken all the hurt, anger, guilt, and frustrations from you. And you no longer have the pain and anguish that comes from harboring them in your heart."

Then I replied, "Lord, let me dwell in your presence forever. Let me stay with you."

He replied, "No, you cannot abide here. You have work that needs to be completed. You're not doing this for the people or for your wife. You're not even doing it for the children. You're doing it for me."

Suddenly I became aware of my surroundings again. I was still holding Dinesha's hands. She smiled. Her tears vanished. The past few moments were like a dream, but I knew that Jesus had touched my heart.

I realized that no one is ever totally free from the past. We are all imprisoned by the phantoms in our boxes. But when Jesus said, "Be whole," I became whole. I still have the scars in my heart, but the pain completely disappeared.

Dinesha could not hide her deformity, nor can I hide mine from God. She will always be a reminder. All of us are hurting, but God loves us and accepts us where we are.

I remembered how I had grown up in a poor southern family and had experienced real hunger as a child. I knew what it meant to be cold and not have enough clothing. Through the eyes of Dinesha, once again, I realized the driving force that had caused me to give up my successful construction business for the children of Sri Lanka.

Chapter Thirteen

A Luncheon to Remember

Memories flooded my mind while I drove along the familiar driveway leading to Colton's house. I parked the car and crossed the fence that separated Colton's manicured lawn from the community of shanties next door. Lallani and Gongala still lived in this village with their parents. However, their home had changed dramatically since our first visit nine years before. The family had added several rooms and a red-tile roof. They had also purchased some crudely-crafted chairs and tables.

When I arrived, I saw the girls standing by the door. Gongala rushed up and threw her arms around me. I had not seen her in almost a year. She was several inches taller.

Lallani gracefully walked up to me. She said softly, "I've missed you, Uncle Deo."

Her beauty astonished me. "I've missed you, too." I put an arm around each girl. We walked back to the van where Elaine waited to greet them.

We planned a special day of shopping, culminating with lunch at a hotel in downtown Colombo. Over the years these two girls had become an important part of our lives. As we traveled along the narrow ribbon of highway leading to town, I recalled the first luncheon date spent with Lallani and Gongala at this same hotel dining room.

On that first outing we arrived in our van as we did today. However, at that time, the young girls had never before ridden in a car. They walked around the car in circles, peeking into each window.

After several minutes I said, "Climb in the back seat. Let's go for a ride."

They giggled to each other. I opened the door, and Gongala jumped onto the seat. Upon discovering the springs, she bounced up and down until the novelty wore off. Lallani slid in next to her.

As we weaved in and out of the traffic, neither girl spoke a word, not knowing how to react to this first automobile ride.

They were then wearing outfits we had purchased on a previous shopping trip. Six-year-old Gongala wore a red pleated skirt, white blouse, and sandals. Red barrettes held back her thick, black hair. Lallani dressed in a ruffled blue dress. Her long, shiny hair was pulled back in a ponytail and tied with a matching blue bow.

Since the Sri Lankan custom is to serve lunch at two or three in the afternoon, we took the girls shopping for a couple of hours. Elaine enjoyed buying clothes for them. They chatted excitedly with each new purchase. Finally our driver arrived and piled the packages in the back of the van.

When we pulled into the circular driveway of the hotel, a doorman opened the car door for the girls. Lallani gracefully stepped out onto the sidewalk. However, Gongala tripped on the curb. She blushed when the doorman caught her.

The ornate, golden doors opened automatically, beckoning us to enter the hotel lobby. Lallani stared at the huge double doors. She hesitated before walking inside.

We remembered how the girls chattered to each other about the coolness of the lobby. The concept of air conditioning was beyond their imaginations. Rubbing her arms, Lallani asked, "Why is it cold in here?"

I did not know how to explain air conditioning in terms

she would comprehend, but I tried. "The hotel owns a big machine that cools the air similar to the way the ocean water cools the breeze that blows inland."

Her puzzled expression told me that my explanation had not helped.

Meanwhile, Gongala walked around the lobby, scooting her sandals across the plush, red carpeting. She giggled and said, "The fur tickles my toes."

Ten stories of balconies opened into the center courtyard lobby. Beautiful hanging plants and creeping vines cascaded from the banisters, forming squares around an atrium filled with tropical plants.

Gongala tilted her head back and tried to see the ceiling. A puzzled expression covered her face. She asked, "How can plants grow inside? How can rain fall on them?"

I thought perhaps I could explain this better than the air conditioning. "People water the plants with jugs, so they can grow."

Once again Gongala stared at the abundant foliage with her large, round eyes. "Why don't they leave the plants outside where they belong?"

Elaine replied, "Girls, don't you think the plants add to the beauty of the lobby? I think they create a garden atmosphere inside where we can enjoy the comfort of air conditioning."

I was not sure the young girls were ready for an elevator ride, so I guided them in the direction of the stairs. They chattered to themselves as we climbed the flights of stairs.

When they entered the restaurant, Gongala pointed to the silverware. Probably, the only utensil she had seen before was a knife. The girls helped their mother cut fish and vegetables, but a fork and spoon were foreign objects. Most Sri Lankans eat with their fingers.

After we were seated, I looked at the menu and asked, "What would you like to eat?"

Neither girl answered. Lallani's eyes darted around the decorated ceiling, then landed on the massive, crystal chandelier. Gongala kept staring at her knife, fork, and spoon.

I ordered soft drinks for them. The pop tickled their tongues when they sipped it. Lallani laughed. Gongala remained silent, looking determined to win the battle with the effervescent substance.

Finally Lallani said, "I like chicken." Gongala nodded in agreement.

We ordered chicken in a basket with a fried banana, french fries, and lime to season it. Elaine and I decided to eat the same thing so the girls would feel more comfortable.

The chicken-filled baskets arrived. The girls looked at us and stared at the baskets. Then they looked at each other, giggling softly. They still did not know what to do with the silverware.

I picked up the chicken with my fingers. Elaine followed my example, motioning to the children to do the same thing. The waiters and local customers watched us, probably wondering what the crazy foreigners would do next. However, our only concern was the two little girls, not what others were thinking.

Lallani took a bite of chicken. Then she whispered in her sister's ear. Gongala kept tilting her head upward, staring at the electric chandelier and the glitter on the gilded ceiling. Neither girl ate her meal.

I remembered the first time I had entered the girls' small hut. I felt overwhelmed by the poverty and living standards. Perhaps they felt a similar reaction in reverse. Air conditioning, indoor plants, fountains, silverware, and electricity were not part of their everyday surroundings. This elegant hotel bewildered the young girls.

I knew they liked ice cream because we had bought cones one day on the street. I ordered small dishes of ice cream for dessert. They conquered the use of the spoon and enjoyed their ice cream.

When I asked the waiter for doggie bags, his expression told me this service was not normally available in Sri

Lanka. The food that is not eaten is taken home to families by the kitchen help or devoured on the spot by the dishwasher and bus boys. They did not care if the rice was half eaten. Someone would finish all that remained on a plate.

Looking puzzled, the waiter inquired, "What are you going to do with the food?"

I explained that the girls were not hungry, but wanted to snack on their chicken later. The waiter brought each girl a box tied with a string in which to carry home her meal. When we rose to leave, Gongala looped her box over her arm and skipped out the door.

Upon reaching home, Gongala ran to her mother with the little box swinging from her arm. She chattered about the chicken, the restaurant, and the ice cream. This was her first encounter with life outside her own village.

Lallani said, "Thank you, Uncle Deo. Thank you, Aunt Elaine. I had a fun day."

On that day, Elaine and I had looked at each other and smiled. The luncheon formed a memory I would never forget.

"Here we are, and am I ever hungry." Elaine's words brought me back to the present time. The hotel doorman opened the van's door. I looked at the two teenagers and thought of how they had changed since our first visit to this same restaurant years ago.

Entering the hotel, we rode the elevator up to the restaurant and were seated. Gongala, bubbling over with enthusiasm, talked on and on. "I'm a senior in high school now. I bought three new textbooks with the money you sent me last month. See my new red dress. I bought it for this special occasion."

I recalled the red, pleated skirt she wore at our first luncheon. Gongala had changed from a small six-year-old to a typical teenager. Yet, I still saw traces of the wide-eyed sparkle that she possessed as a little girl.

My eyes moved to Lallani—quiet, beautiful Lallani. Of

all the children that we touched in the years of our ministry, Lallani reached the deepest into my heart.

She began speaking. "I graduated from high school last year. Now I'm learning accounting through a tutor. Soon I'll finish my internship and find my first full-time job."

"That's exciting, Lallani. Aunt Elaine and I are proud of you."

"Thank you for all the support you have given to me, Uncle Deo. Soon you will no longer need to send me money. I'll be able to pay for all my own food and personal belongings and help Ami and Dad a little, too."

I stared at the beautiful, poised woman before me. I could not believe she was the same little girl who had once told me through a quivering lip, "I'll never see you again, Uncle Deo. I must stay with you until the end."

Little did I realize at that time what an impact Lallani would have on my life and ministry. When we left Sri Lanka after our first visit, we did not know that we would return again and again.

Lallani reached into her purse and brought out a small Bible. She opened the worn New Testament and handed it to me. I flipped through the pages and noticed the underlining and writing in the margins. I stopped at 1 Peter 4:10 and read: "As each one has received a gift, minister it to one another, as good stewards of the manifold grace of God."

I recognized the handwriting in some places as my own. But in other locations, there were verses marked by a different hand. These notes were Lallani's.

"Remember when you gave me this little Bible?" she asked.

A lump formed in my throat and choked my words. All I could do was nod dumbly and stare at the little book before me. Memories of the day I handed the Bible to Lallani flooded my mind.

"I didn't let my parents sell it, and I've learned many of the stories of Jesus. I read my Bible every night before I go to bed. You have given me more than material gifts, Uncle

Deo. You have given me Jesus. Although you won't have to support me financially anymore, I'll always feel your spiritual support. Where I am, you and Jesus will be there, too."

I reached over and squeezed her hand tightly.

The next week Elaine and I returned to California. I set the suitcases down in the entryway of our home. Then I walked into the kitchen and opened the door to the freezer compartment of the refrigerator. My hand slid past the frozen food to a small, crinkled item located at the very back. I reverently removed the precious package and opened it.

Inside lay the three remaining small cubes of brown sugar and ginger. I squeezed them in my palm for a few seconds, wrapping the warmth of my hand around the frozen cubes. Then I carefully laid them back on the worn paper and rewrapped them tightly. Opening the freezer door, I replaced the cherished possession, given to me by a nine-year-old girl so long ago.

Chapter Fourteen

Swamani, the Answer

"Why is your ministry so successful?" people ask wherever I speak. I believe it is because Hope Child Care International Ministries, the work Elaine and I began, is built by people. We are not part of a large organization, nor do we have any individual donors who provide the bulk of the finances. The money to feed the thousands of children in our centers arrives in small envelopes from people all over the United States. At the end of each month, the funds are always sufficient to cover expenses.

Once when our finances were short, a large donation arrived from a sponsor who had sold his house. Another time, a woman wrote, "My business has prospered this month, and I want to share the profits with the children."

Another letter stated, "I have difficulty identifying with large organizations that cannot tell me exactly where my money goes. I know that you will personally take the currency to Sri Lanka to distribute among the churches involved in the feeding and vocational programs for the children."

Some sponsors have been involved from the beginning of our ministry. One person said, "I now have pictures of ninety-six different children. I think of them as my family. I pray for them and I care for them."

Each month a newsletter is sent to everyone supporting our ministry to tell them about the children's activities and needs. A color snapshot of a child is included to give the sponsors an opportunity to pray for one young person. Last month's picture was of Dharshini, a twelve-year-old girl who recently finished her first major needlework project. In the picture she proudly displayed her beautiful lace tablecloth, representing eight months of work.

Money does not always buy life. Yet, we can feed, clothe, and teach a vocation to these children, ultimately bringing them to God. Sponsoring churches and individuals in the United States provide the money to be distributed among the churches for the vocational training and feeding programs. Then, the Sri Lankan people take over the work. The center directors, teachers, and cooks are all native Sri Lankans, proud of their heritage and culture. Working through them, more is accomplished than could be done by an outside agency.

The film donated by World Concern has generated commitments in many hearts. One woman wrote, "I have been your sponsor since I first saw the film. I pray every day for the children. May God bless them and you."

Another person said, "Since I started sponsoring a child monthly in Sri Lanka, I have been unbelievably blessed by God. This year, I will increase my contribution to feed and clothe two children participating in your program."

The promises to take care of little girls and boys whom these sponsors will probably never see are made to God, not to me personally. I never take credit for anything that has happened. All the glory belongs to God, and He always provides enough money to sustain the program. Neither Elaine nor I could have anticipated or planned the tremendous growth of our ministry.

One of my favorite sayings is "Pity comes, sees the need, and walks on by. Compassion comes to help and stays."

When I first found that little girl, abandoned by the side of the road, I knew I could not leave her there to die of starvation. I heard God calling me. Feeding one little girl a day for the price of a cup of coffee was a simple task.

I look back to the time when I was a building contractor. Doubts and fears filled my mind when God first called me to this ministry. Yet, I responded, "I will go where you want me to go. I will be what you want me to be, Lord."

Most of us have gone through times when our lives have been shattered into a thousand pieces. God gives us the choice. We can remain on the ground—shattered, bored, hopeless, questioning, rationalizing. Perhaps we do nothing because the problem looks too big, or we feel our part does not count. Or we can allow the Master Craftsman to mold and reshape us again and use us for His purposes. But the decision is ours.

The stained glass windows of the majestic cathedrals of the world are examples of what can be done with boxes of broken glass. God wants each of us to be the unique person He created us to be. He wants us to allow Him to pick up the fractured slivers of our lives and transform them into whole panes of glass once again, creating a magnificent stained glass window. God places each fragment of glass in the perfect place He has chosen. Each segment of glass depends on every other part to complete the picture. It takes God to hold us together.

The children in the feeding and vocational programs represent many fragments of glass. Lallani, Gongala, Surakata, and Dinesha are all precious segments of glass, polished and lovingly placed in the window. Elaine and I are also pieces of the transformed glass. Other multicolored pieces are the supporters, combining to reach out and touch the children. All join to form the whole.

To be complete, the window needs all of us. Without our part some segments of glass won't conform. Each individual part is necessary.

God's method is people, ordinary people, interconnecting with one another to build the stained glass window. Our window is built as high as possible without adding other shattered fragments of glass. Perhaps you are the next piece for which we have been waiting and praying.

Numerous TV and radio programs continue to open doors for our ministry. Elaine's fashion shows provide more needed funding. Yet, I doubt that work among the children will ever be completed. More could be done if additional individuals were willing to join us.

The Sinhala word for Lord is Swamani. Jesus visited many towns where He was greeted by children who followed Him, listening to His words. Today, Elaine and I are met by children who come running at each village we visit. These young ones open many doors for us to share Jesus and His love with our friends and families. We are ambassadors bringing the answer—Swamani—to the children of Sri Lanka.

People ask me, "What is the greatest reward you receive from your ministry?"

When I visit the vocational centers, my reward lies in the eyes of the children. Instead of the haunting brown eyes that filled my mind after my first trip to Sri Lanka, I now see peaceful eyes filled with love. I no longer envision a look of fear and pain coupled with thinning, ginger-colored hair and distended stomachs. Now, I see shiny hair, sparkling teeth, and healthy bodies. The children still play in the dirt and look a bit ragged, but they are alive and healthy.

The reflection of God's love in their eyes tells the whole story. A boy named Rattan summed up his feelings by saying, "Thank you. Thank you for giving me the opportunity to grow up healthy, to learn a trade, and to personally come to know Jesus as my Savior. Without you, it would not have been possible."

Jesus said, "For I was hungry and you gave Me food; I was thirsty and you gave Me drink; I was a stranger and you took me in; I was was naked and you clothed Me; I was sick and you visited Me; I was in prison and you came to Me. . . . Assuredly, I say to you, inasmuch as you did it to one of the least of these My brethren, you did it to Me" (Matt. 25:35–40).

Over the past years, we have watched many children grow up and find jobs, using the skills taught in the vocational centers. They return to say thank you. Many, like Lallani and Gongala, will someday become independent individuals. We lose touch with some, as we have the little girl found by the side of the road. We never know their fates, and there are hundreds of girls and boys who have taken their places. Yet, thousands remain, standing outside the feeding center gates, waiting for someone to come along and pick up the pieces of their fragmented lives.

To touch a child's spirit with the love of Jesus is the ministry that brings eternal life. Evidence of this eternal life is portrayed in a child's eyes as they reflect the light and love of Jesus.

Next time you are in a church, look carefully at the stained glass windows. Picture yourself as part of His magnificent stained glass window. Watch the sun piercing through each unique piece of glass. Notice how many shapes and sizes are necessary to form the whole.

Remember that the Master Craftsman started with one—one piece of fractured glass. What can we accomplish for His glory if we, too, start with one?

About the Ministry

If you are interested
in receiving further information on
Hope Child Care International Ministries,
please write:

Deo Miller
P.O. Box 874
Walnut, California 91789